COACHING YOUTH

HOCKEY

American Sport Education Program

With Huron Ice and Roller Hockey Schools

Human Kinetics

Library of Congress Cataloging-in-Publication Data

Coaching youth hockey/ American Sport Education Program with Huron
Ice and Roller Hockey Schools.
    p.   cm.
    ISBN 0-87322-964-9 (trade paper)
    1. Hockey--Coaching.   2. Roller hockey.   I. American Sport
Education Program.   II. Huron Ice and Roller Hockey Schools.
GV848.25.C63   1996
796.962'07'7--dc20   95-34844
                                                                 CIP

ISBN: 0-87322-964-9

Acquisitions Editor: Jim Kestner; **Hockey Consultant:** Wayne Anderson; **Devel-
opmental Editor:** Jan Colarusso Seeley; **Assistant Editor:** Erin Cler; **Editorial Assistant:** Andrew Starr; **Copyeditor:** Jim Kestner; **Proofreader:** Kathy Bennett; **Type-
setter and Layout Artist:** Francine Hamerski; **Text Designer:** Judy Henderson; **Cover
Designer:** Stuart Cartwright; **Photographer (cover):** Dave Black; **Illustrators:** Tim
Stiles, cartoons; Tim Offenstein, line drawings; and Jennifer Delmotte, Mac art;
Printer: United Graphics

Printed in the United States of America   10   9   8   7   6   5   4   3   2   1

Human Kinetics
P.O. Box 5076, Champaign, IL 61825-5076
1-800-747-4457

Canada: Human Kinetics, Box 24040, Windsor, ON N8Y 4Y9
1-800-465-7301 (in Canada only)

Europe: Human Kinetics, P.O. Box IW14, Leeds LS16 6TR, United Kingdom
(44) 1132 781708

Australia: Human Kinetics, 2 Ingrid Street, Clapham 5062, South Australia
(08) 371 3755

New Zealand: Human Kinetics, P.O. Box 105-231, Auckland 1
(09) 523 3462

Contents

Coaching young people is an exciting way to be involved in sport. But it isn't easy. The untrained novice coach may be overwhelmed by the responsibilities involved in helping athletes through their early sport experiences. Preparing youngsters physically and mentally in their sport and providing them with a positive role model are among the difficult—but rewarding—tasks you will assume as a coach.

This book will help you meet the challenges and experience the rewards of coaching young athletes. We call it *Coaching Youth Hockey* because it is intended for coaches who are working with developing ice and roller hockey players. In this book you'll learn how to apply general coaching principles and teach ice and roller hockey rules, skills, and strategies successfully to kids. This book also serves as a text for the American Sport Education Program's (ASEP) Rookie Coaches Course.

We hope you will find coaching rewarding and that you will continue to learn more about coaching and your sport so that you can be the best possible coach for your young athletes.

If you would like more information about ASEP and its Rookie Coaches Course, please contact us at

ASEP
P.O. Box 5076
Champaign, IL 61825-5076
1-800-747-5698

Good Coaching!

Unit 1

Who, Me . . . a Coach?

If you are like most rookie coaches, you have probably been recruited from the ranks of concerned parents, sport enthusiasts, or community volunteers. And, like many rookie and veteran coaches, you probably have had little formal instruction on how to coach. But when the call went out for coaches to assist with the local youth hockey program, you answered because you like children and enjoy hockey, and perhaps because you want to be involved in a worthwhile community activity.

I Want to Help, but . . .

Your initial coaching assignment may be difficult. Like many volunteers, you may not know much about the sport you have agreed to coach or about how to work with children between the ages of 6 and 14. Relax, because *Coaching Youth Hockey* will help you find the answers to such common questions as these:

- What do I need to be a good coach?
- How can I best communicate with my players?
- How do I go about teaching sport skills?
- What can I do to promote safety?
- What should I do when someone is injured?
- What are the basic rules, skills, and strategies of hockey?
- What practice drills will improve my players' hockey skills?

Before answering these questions, let's take a look at what's involved in being a coach.

Am I a Parent or a Coach?

Many coaches are parents, but the two roles should not be confused. Unlike your role as a parent, as a coach you are responsible not only to yourself and your child, but also to the organization, all the players on the team (including your child), and their parents. Because of this additional responsibility, your behavior on the rink will be different from your behavior at home, and your son or daughter may not understand why.

For example, imagine the confusion of a young boy who is the center of his parents' attention at home but is barely noticed by his father/ coach in the sport setting. Or consider the mixed signals received by a young girl whose hockey skill is constantly evaluated by a mother/ coach who otherwise rarely comments on her daughter's activities. You need to explain to your son or daughter your new responsibilities and how they will affect your relationship when coaching.

Take the following steps to avoid such problems in coaching your child:

- Ask your child if he or she wants you to coach the team.
- Explain why you wish to be involved with the team.
- Discuss how your interactions will change when you take on the role of coach at practice or games.
- Limit your coaching behavior to when you are in the coaching role.

- Avoid parenting during practice or game situations, to keep your role clear in your child's mind.
- Reaffirm your love for your child, irrespective of his or her performance on the hockey rink.

What Are My Responsibilities as a Coach?

A coach assumes the responsibility of doing everything possible to ensure that the youngsters on his or her team will have an enjoyable and safe sporting experience while they learn sport skills.

Provide an Enjoyable Experience

Sport should be fun. Even if nothing else is accomplished, make certain your players have fun. Take the fun out of sport and you'll take the kids out of sport.

Children enter sport for a number of reasons (e.g., to meet and play with other children, to develop physically, and to learn skills), but their major objective is to have fun. Help them satisfy this goal by injecting humor and variety into your practices. Also, make games nonthreatening, festive experiences for your players. Such an approach will increase your players' desire to participate in the future, which should be the biggest goal of youth sport. Unit 2 will help you learn how to satisfy your players' yearning for fun and keep winning in perspective. And unit 3 will describe how you can effectively communicate this perspective to them.

Provide a Safe Experience

You are responsible for planning and teaching activities in such a way that the progression between activities minimizes risks (see units 4 and 5). Further, you must ensure that the facility at which your team practices and plays and the equipment team members use are free of hazards. Finally, you need to protect yourself from any legal liability that might arise from your involvement as a coach. Unit 5 will help you take the appropriate precautions.

Provide Opportunities for Children With Disabilities

There's a possibility that a child with a disability of some kind will register for your team. Don't panic! Your youth sport administrator or a number of organizations (see Appendix A) can provide you with information to help you best meet this child's needs.

As a coach, you need to know about the Americans with Disabilities Act (ADA). Passed in 1990, the ADA gives individuals with disabilities the same legal protection against discrimination on the basis of disabilities as is provided against discrimination on such bases as race, gender, and class. The law does recognize that there are times when including an individual who is disabled might risk the safety of that individual and other players, but the exact way that courts are treating the ADA is still being decided. In general, the law requires that "reasonable accommodations" be made to include children with disabilities into organized sport programs. If a parent or child approaches you on the subject, and you aren't sure what to do, talk to the director in charge of your hockey program. If you make any decision on your own pertaining to the ADA, you may be vulnerable to a lawsuit.

Keep in mind that these children want to participate alongside their able-bodied peers. Give them the same support and encouragement that you give other athletes, and model their inclusion and acceptance for all your athletes.

Teach Basic Hockey Skills

In becoming a coach, you take on the role of educator. You must teach your players the fundamental skills and strategies necessary for success in their sport. That means that you need to "go to school."

If you don't know the basics of hockey now, you can learn them by reading the second half of this manual, units 6, 7, and 8. But even if you know hockey as a player, do you know how to teach it? This book will help you get started. There are also many valuable hockey books on the market, including those offered by Human Kinetics. See the information in the back of this book or call 1-800-747-4457 for more information.

You'll also find it easier to provide good educational experiences for your players if you plan your practices. Unit 4 of this manual provides some guidelines for the planning process.

Getting Help

Veteran coaches in your league are an especially good source of help for you. They have all experienced the same emotions and concerns you are facing, and their advice can be invaluable as you work through your first season.

You can get additional help by watching hockey coaches in practices and games, attending workshops, reading hockey publications, and studying instructional videos. In addition to the American Sport Education Program (ASEP), the following national organizations will assist you in obtaining more hockey coaching information:

Roller Hockey

International In-Line Skating Association
P.O. Box 15482
Atlanta, GA 30333
(404) 728-9707

National In-Line Hockey Association
999 Brickell Ave., 9th Fl.
Miami, FL 33131
(800) 358-NIHA

Roller Hockey International
5182 Katella Ave., #106
Los Alamitos, CA 90720
(310) 430-2423

United States Amateur Confederation of Roller Skating
4730 South St.
Lincoln, NE 68506
(402) 483-7551

USA Hockey Inline
(a division of USA Hockey)
4965 N. 30th St.
Colorado Springs, CO 80919
(800) 566-3288

Ice Hockey

USA Hockey
4965 N. 30th St.
Colorado Springs, CO 80919
(800) 566-3288

Hockey Development Center for Ontario
1185 Eglinton Ave. East, Suite 301
North York, Ontario M3C 3C6
(416) 426-7252

Canadian Amateur Hockey Association
Suite 607, 1600 James Naismith Dr.
Gloucester, Ontario K1B 5N4
(613) 748-5613

Coaching hockey is a rewarding experience. And your players will be rewarded if you learn all you can about coaching so you can be the best hockey coach you can be.

What Tools Do I Need as a Coach?

Have you purchased the traditional coaching tools—things like whistles, coaching clothes, ice or in-line skates, and a clipboard? They'll help you coach, but to be a successful coach you'll need five other tools that cannot be bought. These tools are available only through self-examination and hard work; they're easy to remember with the acronym COACH:

> C—Comprehension
>
> O—Outlook
>
> A—Affection
>
> C—Character
>
> H—Humor

Comprehension

Comprehension of the rules, skills, and tactics of hockey is required. It is essential that you understand the basic elements of the sport. To assist you in learning about the game, the second half of this guide describes rules, skills, and tactics. In the hockey-specific section of this book, you'll also find a variety of drills to use in developing young players' skills.

To improve your comprehension of hockey, take the following steps:

- Read the hockey-specific section of this book.
- Consider reading other hockey coaching books, including those available from ASEP (see pages 177 and 178 to order).
- Contact any of the organizations listed on page 7.
- Attend hockey clinics and coaches clinics.
- Talk with other, more experienced, coaches.
- Observe local college, high school, and youth hockey games.
- Watch hockey games on television.

In addition to having hockey knowledge, you must implement proper training and safety methods so your players can participate with little risk of injury. Even then, sport injuries will occur. And more often than not, you'll be the first person responding to your players' injuries, so be sure you understand the basic emergency care procedures described in unit 5. Also, read in that unit how to handle more serious sport injury situations.

Outlook

Outlook refers to your perspective and goals—what you are seeking as a coach. The most common coaching objectives are (a) to have fun, (b) to help players develop their physical, mental, and social skills, and (c) to win. Thus your outlook involves the priorities you set, your planning, and your vision for the future.

To work successfully with children in a sport setting, you must have your priorities in order. In just what order do you rank the importance of fun, development, and winning?

Answer the following questions to examine your objectives:

Of which situation would you be most proud?

    a. Knowing that each participant enjoyed playing hockey.

    b. Seeing that all players improved their hockey skills.

    c. Winning the league championship.

Which statement best reflects your thoughts about sport?

    a. If it isn't fun, don't do it.

    b. Everyone should learn something every day.

    c. Sports aren't fun if you don't win.

How would you like your players to remember you?

    a. As a coach who was fun to play for.

    b. As a coach who provided a good base of fundamental skills.

    c. As a coach who had a winning record.

Which would you most like to hear a parent of a child on your team say?

    a. Billy really had a good time playing hockey this year.

    b. Susie learned some important lessons playing hockey this year.

    c. Jose played on the first-place hockey team this year.

Which of the following would be the most rewarding moment of your season?

    a. Having your team wanting to continue playing, even after practice is over.

    b. Seeing one of your players finally master the skill of stick handling without constantly looking at the puck/ball.

    c. Winning the league championship.

Look over your answers. If you most often selected "a" responses, then having fun is most important to you. A majority of "b" answers suggests that skill development is what attracts you to coaching. And if "c" was your most frequent response, winning is tops on your list of coaching priorities.

Most coaches say fun and development are more important, but when actually coaching, some coaches emphasize—indeed overemphasize—winning. You, too, will face situations that challenge you to keep winning in its proper perspective. During such moments, you'll have to choose between emphasizing your players' development or winning. If your priorities are in order, your players' well-being will take precedence over your team's win-loss record every time.

Take the following actions to better define your outlook:

1. Determine your priorities for the season.

2. Prepare for situations that challenge your priorities.

3. Set goals for yourself and your players that are consistent with those priorities.

4. Plan how you and your players can best attain those goals.

5. Review your goals frequently to be sure that you are staying on track.

It is particularly important for coaches to permit all young athletes to participate. Each youngster—male and female, small and tall, gifted and disabled—should have an opportunity to develop skills and have fun.

Remember that the challenge and joy of sport is experienced through striving to win, not through winning itself. Players who aren't allowed off the bench are denied the opportunity to strive to win. And herein lies the irony: Coaches who allow all of their players to participate and develop skills will—in the end—come out on top.

ASEP has a motto that will help you keep your outlook in the best interest of the kids on your team. It summarizes in four words all you need to remember when establishing your coaching priorities:

Athletes First,
Winning Second

This motto recognizes that striving to win is an important, even vital, part of sport. But it emphatically states that no efforts in striving to win should be made at the expense of the well-being, development, and enjoyment of the athletes.

Affection

Affection is another vital tool you will want to have in your coaching kit: a genuine concern for the young people you coach. It involves having a love for children, a desire to share with them your love and knowledge of hockey, and the patience and understanding that allow each individual playing for you to grow from his or her involvement in sport.

Successful coaches have a real concern for the health and welfare of their players. They care that each child on the team has an enjoyable and successful experience. They recognize that there are similarities between young people's sport experiences and other activities in their lives, and they encourage their players to strive to learn from all their experiences, to become well-rounded individuals. These coaches have a strong desire to work with children and be involved in their growth. And they have the patience to work with those who are slower to learn or less capable of performing. If you have such qualities or are willing to work hard to develop them, then you have the affection necessary to coach young athletes.

There are many ways to demonstrate your affection and patience, including these:

- Make an effort to get to know each player on your team.
- Treat each player as an individual.
- Empathize with players trying to learn new and difficult sport skills.
- Treat players as you would like to be treated under similar circumstances.
- Be in control of your emotions.
- Show your enthusiasm for being involved with your team.
- Keep an upbeat and positive tone in all of your communications.

Some children appreciate a pat on the back or shoulder as a sign of your approval or affection. But be aware that not all players feel comfortable with being touched. When this is the case, you need to respect their wishes.

Character

Character is a word that adults use frequently in conversations about sport experiences and young people. If you haven't already, you may one day be asked to explain whether you think sport builds good character. What will you say?

The fact that you have decided to coach young hockey players probably means that you think participation in sport is important. But whether or not that participation develops character in your players depends as much on you as it does the sport itself. How can you build character in your players?

Youngsters learn by listening to what adults say. But they learn even more by watching the behavior of certain important individuals. As a coach, you are likely to be a significant figure in the lives of your players. Will you be a good role model?

Having good character means modeling appropriate behaviors for sport and life. That means more than just saying the right things. What you say and what you do must match. There is no place in coaching for the "Do as I say, not as I do" philosophy. Challenge, support, encourage, and reward every child, and your players will be more likely to accept, even celebrate, their differences. Be in control before, during, and after all games and practices. And don't be afraid to admit that you were wrong. No one is perfect!

Many of us have been coached by someone who believes that criticizing players is a good way to build character. In reality, this approach damages children's self-esteem and teaches them that their value as a person is based on how they perform in sport. Unit 3 will help you communicate with your players in a way that builds positive self-esteem and develops your athletes' skills.

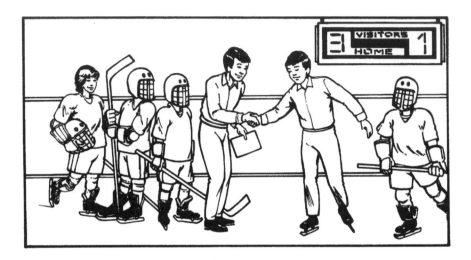

Finally, take stock of your own attitudes about ethnic, gender, and other stereotypes. You are an individual coach, and it would be wrong for others to form beliefs about you based on their personal attitudes about coaches in general. Similarly, you need to avoid making comments that support stereotypes of others. Let your words and actions show your players that every individual matters, and you will be teaching them a valuable lesson about respecting and supporting individuals' differences.

Consider the following steps to being a good role model:

- Take stock of your strengths and weaknesses.
- Build on your strengths.
- Set goals for yourself to improve upon those areas you would not like to see mimicked.
- If you slip up, apologize to your team and to yourself. You'll do better next time.

Humor

Humor is an often-overlooked coaching tool. For our use it means having the ability to laugh at yourself and with your players during practices and games. Nothing helps balance the tone of a serious, skill-learning session like a chuckle or two. And a sense of humor puts in perspective the many mistakes your young players will make. So don't get upset over each miscue or respond negatively to erring players. Allow your players and yourself to enjoy the ups, and don't dwell on the downs.

Here are some tips for injecting humor into your practices:

- Make practices fun by including a variety of activities.
- Keep all players involved in drills and scrimmages.
- Consider laughter by your players a sign of enjoyment, not waning discipline.
- Smile!

Where Do You Stand?

To take stock of your "coaching tool kit," rank yourself on the three questions for each of the five coaching tools. Simply circle the number that best describes your current status on each item.

Not at all		Somewhat		Very much so
1	2	3	4	5

Comprehension

1. Could you explain the rules of hockey to other parents without studying for a long time?   1 2 3 4 5

2. Do you know how to organize and conduct safe hockey practices?   1 2 3 4 5

3. Do you know how to provide first aid for most common, minor sport injuries?   1 2 3 4 5

Comprehension Score: _____

Outlook _____

4.	Do you place the interests of all children ahead of winning when you coach?	1 2 3 4 5
5.	Do you plan for every meeting and practice?	1 2 3 4 5
6.	Do you have a vision of what you want your players to be able to do by the end of the season?	1 2 3 4 5

Outlook Score: _____

Affection _____

7.	Do you enjoy working with children?	1 2 3 4 5
8.	Are you patient with youngsters learning new skills?	1 2 3 4 5
9.	Are you able to show your players that you care?	1 2 3 4 5

Affection Score: _____

Character _____

10.	Are your words and behaviors consistent with each other?	1 2 3 4 5
11.	Are you a good model for your players?	1 2 3 4 5
12.	Do you keep negative emotions under control before, during, and after matches?	1 2 3 4 5

Character Score: _____

Humor _____

13.	Do you usually smile at your players?	1 2 3 4 5
14.	Are your practices fun?	1 2 3 4 5
15.	Are you able to laugh at your mistakes?	1 2 3 4 5

Humor Score: _____

If you scored 9 or less on any of the coaching tools, be sure to reread those sections carefully. And even if you scored 15 on each tool, don't be complacent. Keep learning! Then you'll be well-equipped with the tools you need to coach young athletes.

Now you know the tools needed to COACH: Comprehension, Outlook, Affection, Character, and Humor. These are essentials for effective coaching; without them, you'd have a difficult time getting started. But none of those tools will work if you don't know how to use them with your athletes—and this requires skillful communication. This unit examines what communication is and how you can become a more effective communicator-coach.

What's Involved in Communication?

Coaches often mistakenly believe that communication involves only instructing players to do something, but verbal commands are a very small part of the communication process. More than half of what is communicated is nonverbal. So remember when you are coaching: Actions speak louder than words.

Communication in its simplest form involves two people: a sender and a receiver. The sender transmits the message verbally, through facial expression, and possibly through body language. Once the message is sent, the receiver must assimilate it successfully. A receiver who fails to attend or listen will miss parts, if not all, of the message.

How Can I Send More Effective Messages?

Young athletes often have little understanding of the rules and skills of hockey and probably even less confidence in playing it. So they need accurate, understandable, and supportive messages to help them along. That's why your verbal and nonverbal messages are so important.

Verbal Messages

"Sticks and stones may break my bones, but words will never hurt me" isn't true. Spoken words can have a strong and long-lasting effect. And coaches' words are particularly influential because youngsters place great importance on what coaches say. Perhaps you, like many former youth sport participants, have a difficult time remembering much of anything you were told by your elementary school teachers but can still recall several specific things your coaches at that level said to you. Such is the lasting effect of a coach's comments to a player.

Whether you are correcting misbehavior, teaching a player how to hit the puck/ball, or praising a player for good effort, there are a number of things you should consider when sending a message verbally. They include the following:

- *Be positive and honest.*
- *State it clearly and simply.*
- *Say it loud enough, and say it again.*
- *Be consistent.*

Be Positive and Honest

Nothing turns people off like hearing someone nag all the time, and young athletes react similarly to a coach who gripes constantly. Kids particularly need encouragement because they often doubt their ability to perform in sport. So look for and tell your players what they did well.

But don't cover up poor or incorrect play with rosy words of praise. Kids know all too well when they've erred, and no cheerfully expressed cliché can undo their mistakes. If you fail to acknowledge players' errors, your athletes will think you are a phony.

State It Clearly and Simply

Positive and honest messages are good, but only if expressed directly in words your players understand. "Beating around the bush" is ineffective and inefficient. And if you do ramble, your players will miss the point of your message and probably lose interest. Here are some tips for saying things clearly:

- Organize your thoughts before speaking to your athletes.
- Explain things thoroughly, but don't bore them with long-winded monologues.

- Use language your players can understand. However, avoid trying to be hip by using their age group's slang vocabulary.

COMPLIMENT SANDWICH

A good way to handle situations in which you have identified and must correct improper technique is to serve your players a "compliment sandwich":

1. Point out what the athlete did correctly.
2. Let the player know what was incorrect in the performance and instruct him or her how to correct it.
3. Encourage the player by reemphasizing what he or she did well.

Say It Loud Enough, and Say It Again

Talk to your team in a voice that all members can hear and interpret. A crisp, vigorous voice commands attention and respect; garbled and weak speech is tuned out. It's OK, in fact, appropriate, to soften your voice when speaking to a player individually about a personal problem. But most of the time your messages will be for all your players to hear, so make sure they can! An enthusiastic voice also motivates players and tells them you enjoy being their coach. A word of caution, however: Don't dominate the setting with a booming voice that distracts attention from players' performances.

Sometimes what you say, even if stated loud and clear, won't sink in the first time. This may be particularly true with young athletes hearing words they don't understand. To avoid boring repetition and yet still get your message across, say the same thing in a slightly different way. For instance, you might first tell your players "In a one-on-one situation on defense, keep your body between your opponent and the net." Soon afterward, remind them "In a one-on-one situation on defense, watch your opponent's stomach rather than the puck and force the player to the outside." The second form of the message may get through to players who missed it the first time around.

Be Consistent

People often say things in ways that imply a different message. For example, a touch of sarcasm added to the words "way to go" sends an entirely different message than the words themselves suggest. It is essential that you avoid sending such mixed messages. Keep the tone of your voice consistent with the words you use. And don't say something one day and contradict it the next; players will get their wires crossed.

Nonverbal Messages

Just as you should be consistent in the tone of voice and words you use, you should also keep your verbal and nonverbal messages consistent. An extreme example of failing to do this would be shaking your head, indicating disapproval, while at the same time telling a player "Nice try." Which is the player to believe, your gesture or your words?

Messages can be sent nonverbally in a number of ways. Facial expressions and body language are just two of the more obvious forms of nonverbal signals that can help you when you coach.

Facial Expressions

The look on a person's face is the quickest clue to what he or she thinks or feels. Your players know this, so they will study your face, looking for any sign that will tell them more than the words you say. Don't try to fool them by putting on a happy or blank "mask." They'll see through it, and you'll lose credibility.

Serious, stone-faced expressions are no help to kids who need cues as to how they are performing. They will just assume you're unhappy or disinterested. Don't be afraid to smile. A smile from a coach can give a great boost to an unsure young athlete. Plus, a smile lets your players know that you are happy coaching them. But don't overdo it, or your players won't be able to tell when you are genuinely pleased by something they've done or when you are just putting on a smiling face.

Body Language

What would your players think you were feeling if you came to practice slouched over, with head down and shoulders slumped? Tired? Bored? Unhappy? What would they think you were feeling if you watched them during a game with your hands on your hips, your jaws clenched, and your face reddened? Upset with them? Disgusted at an official? Mad at a fan? Probably some or all of these things would enter your players' minds. And none of these impressions is the kind you want your players to have of you. That's why you should carry yourself in a pleasant, confident, and vigorous manner. Such a posture not only projects happiness with your coaching role but also provides a good example for your young players who may model your behavior.

Physical contact can also be a very important use of body language. A handshake, a pat on the head, an arm around the shoulder, or even a big hug are effective ways of showing approval, concern, affection, and joy to your players. Youngsters are especially in need of this type of nonverbal message. Keep within the obvious moral and legal limits, but don't be reluctant to touch your players and send a message that can only truly be expressed in that way.

How Can I Improve My Receiving Skills?

Now, let's examine the other half of the communication process—receiving messages. Too often people are very good senders and very poor receivers of messages. As a coach of young athletes, it is essential that you are able to fulfill both roles effectively.

The requirements for receiving messages are quite simple, but receiving skills are perhaps less satisfying and therefore underdeveloped compared to sending skills. People seem to naturally enjoy hearing themselves talk more than others. But if you are willing to read about the keys to receiving messages and to make a strong effort to use them with your players, you'll be surprised by what you've been missing.

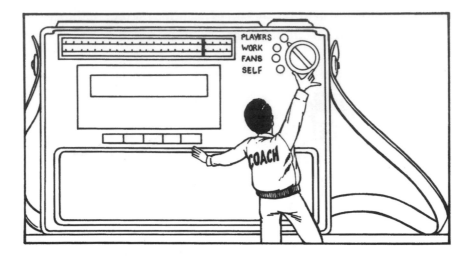

Attention!

First, you must pay attention; you must want to hear what others have to communicate to you. That's not always easy when you're busy coaching and have many things competing for your attention. But in one-to-one or team meetings with players, you must really focus on what they are telling you, both verbally and nonverbally. You'll be amazed at the little signals you pick up. Not only will such focused attention help you catch every word your players say, but you'll also notice your players' moods and physical states, and you'll get an idea of your players' feelings toward you and other players on the team.

Listen CARE-FULLY

How we receive messages from others, perhaps more than anything else we do, demonstrates how much we care for the sender and what that person has to tell us. If you care little for your players or have little regard for what they have to say, it will show in how you attend and listen to them. Check yourself. Do you find your mind wandering to what you are going to do after practice while one of your players is talking to you? Do you frequently have to ask your players "What did you say?" If so, you need to work on your receiving mechanics of attending and listening. But perhaps the most critical question you should ask yourself, if you find that you're missing the messages your players send, is this: Do I care?

How Do I Put It All Together?

So far we've discussed separately the sending and receiving of messages. But we all know that senders and receivers switch roles several times during an interaction. One person initiates a communication by sending a message to another person, who then receives the message. The receiver then switches roles and becomes the sender by responding to the person who sent the initial message. These verbal and nonverbal responses are called feedback.

Your players will be looking to you for feedback all the time. They will want to know how you think they are performing, what you think of their ideas, and whether their efforts please you. Obviously, you can respond in many different ways. How you respond will strongly affect your players. So let's take a look at a few general types of feedback and examine their possible effects.

Providing Instructions

With young players, much of your feedback will involve answering questions about how to play hockey. Your instructive responses to these questions should include both verbal and nonverbal feedback. Here are some suggestions for giving instructional feedback:

- Keep verbal instructions simple and concise.
- Use demonstrations to provide nonverbal instructional feedback (see unit 4).
- "Walk" players through the skill, or use a slow-motion demonstration if they are having trouble learning.

Correcting Errors

When your players perform incorrectly, you need to provide informative feedback to correct the error—and the sooner the better. And when you do correct errors, keep in mind these two principles: Use negative criticism sparingly, and keep calm.

Use Negative Criticism Sparingly

Although you may need to punish players for horseplay or dangerous activities by scolding or removing them from activity temporarily, avoid reprimanding players for performance errors. Admonishing players for honest mistakes makes them afraid to even try. Nothing ruins a youngster's enjoyment of a sport more than a coach who harps on every miscue. So instead, correct your players by using the positive approach. Your players will enjoy playing more, and you'll enjoy coaching more.

Keep Calm

Don't fly off the handle when your players make mistakes. Remember, you're coaching young and inexperienced players, not pros. You'll therefore see more incorrect than correct technique, and you'll probably have more discipline problems than you expect. But throwing a tantrum over each error or misbehavior will only inhibit your players or suggest to them the wrong kind of behavior to model. So let your players know that mistakes aren't the end of the world; stay cool!

Giving Positive Feedback

Praising players when they have performed or behaved well is an effective way of getting them to repeat (or try to repeat) that behavior in the future. And positive feedback for effort is an especially effective way to motivate youngsters to work on difficult skills. So rather than shouting and providing negative feedback to a player who has made a mistake, try offering players a compliment sandwich, described on page 22.

Sometimes just the way you word feedback can make it more positive than negative. For example, instead of saying "Don't pass the puck that way," you might say "Pass the puck this way." Then your players will be focusing on what to do instead of what not to do.

You can give positive feedback verbally and nonverbally. Telling a player, especially in front of teammates, that he or she has performed well, is a great way to boost the confidence of a youngster. And a pat on the back or a handshake can be a very tangible way of communicating your recognition of a player's performance.

Coaches, be positive!

Only a very small percentage of ASEP-trained coaches'
behaviors are negative.

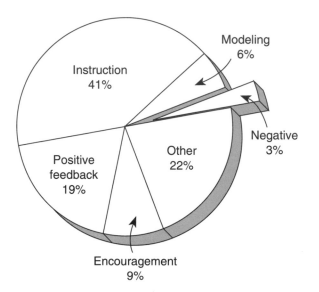

Who Else Do I Need to Communicate With?

Coaching involves not only sending and receiving messages and providing proper feedback to players, but also interacting with parents, fans, game officials, and opposing coaches. If you don't communicate effectively with these groups of people, your coaching career will be unpleasant and short-lived. So try the following suggestions for communicating with these groups.

Parents

A player's parents need to be assured that their son or daughter is under the direction of a coach who is both knowledgeable about the sport and concerned about the youngster's well-being. You can put their worries to rest by holding a preseason parent orientation meeting in which you describe your background and your approach to coaching.

If parents contact you with a concern during the season, listen to them closely and try to offer positive responses. If you need to communicate with parents, catch them after a practice, give them a phone call, or send a note through the mail. Messages sent to parents through children are too often lost, misinterpreted, or forgotten.

Fans

The stands probably won't be overflowing at your games, but that only means that you'll more easily hear the few fans who criticize your coaching. When you hear something negative said about the job you're doing, don't respond. Keep calm, consider whether the message had any value, and if not, forget it. Acknowledging critical, unwarranted comments from a fan during a game will only encourage others to voice their opinions. So put away your "rabbit ears" and communicate to fans, through your actions, that you are a confident, competent coach.

Prepare your players for fans' criticisms. Tell them it is you, not the spectators, to whom they should listen. If you notice that one of your players is rattled by a fan's comment, reassure the player that your evaluation is more objective and favorable—and the one that counts.

Game Officials

How you communicate with officials will have a great influence on the way your players behave toward them. Therefore you need to set an example. Greet officials with a handshake, an introduction, and perhaps some casual conversation about the upcoming game. Indicate your respect for them before, during, and after the game. Don't make nasty remarks, shout, or use disrespectful body gestures. Your players will see you do it, and they'll get the idea that such behavior is appropriate. Plus, if the official hears or sees you, the communication between the two of you will break down.

Opposing Coaches

Make an effort to visit with the coach of the opposing team before the game. Perhaps the two of you can work out a special arrangement for the game, such as no offsides or no penalties. During the game, don't get into a personal feud with the opposing coach. Remember, it's the kids, not the coaches, who are competing. And by getting along well with the opposing coach, you'll show your players that competition involves cooperation.

✔ *Summary Checklist*

Now, check your coach-communication skills by answering "Yes" or "No" to the following questions.

	Yes	No
1. Are your verbal messages to your players positive and honest?	____	____
2. Do you speak loudly, clearly, and in a language your athletes understand?	____	____
3. Do you remember to repeat instructions to your players, in case they didn't hear you the first time?	____	____
4. Are the tone of your voice and your nonverbal messages consistent with the words you use?	____	____
5. Do your facial expressions and body language express interest in and happiness with your coaching role?	____	____
6. Are you attentive to your players and able to pick up even their small verbal and nonverbal cues?	____	____
7. Do you really care about what your athletes say to you?	____	____
8. Do you instruct rather than criticize when your players make errors?	____	____
9. Are you usually positive when responding to things your athletes say and do?	____	____
10. Do you try to communicate in a cooperative and respectful manner with players' parents, fans, game officials, and opposing coaches?	____	____

If you answered "No" to any of the above questions, you may want to refer back to the section of the chapter where the topic was discussed. Now is the time to address communication problems, not when you're coaching young athletes.

To coach hockey, you must understand the basic rules, skills, and strategies of the sport. The second part of this book provides the basic information you'll need to comprehend the sport.

But all the hockey knowledge in the world will do you little good unless you present it effectively to your players. That's why this unit is so important. Here you will learn the steps to take when teaching sport skills, as well as practical guidelines for planning your season and individual practices.

How Do I Teach Sport Skills?

Many people believe that the only qualification needed to coach is to have played the sport. It's helpful to have played, but there is much more to coaching successfully. And even if you haven't played or even watched hockey, you can still learn to coach successfully with this IDEA:

I—Introduce the skill.

D—Demonstrate the skill.

E—Explain the skill.

A—Attend to players practicing the skill.

Introduce the Skill

Players, especially young and inexperienced ones, need to know what skill they are learning and why they are learning it. You should therefore take these three steps every time you introduce a skill to your players:

1. Get your players' attention.
2. Name the skill.
3. Explain the importance of the skill.

Get Your Players' Attention

Because youngsters are easily distracted, use some method to get their attention. Some coaches use interesting news items or stories. Others use jokes. And others simply project enthusiasm that gets their players to listen. Whatever method you use, speak slightly above the normal volume and look your players in the eye when you speak.

Also, position players so they can see and hear you. Arrange the players in two or three evenly spaced rows, facing you and not some source of distraction. Then ask if all can see you before you begin.

Name the Skill

Although you might mention other common names for the skill, decide which one you'll use and stick with it. This will help avoid confusion and enhance communication among your players.

Explain the Importance of the Skill

Although the importance of a skill may be apparent to you, your players may be less able to see how the skill will help them become better hockey players. Offer them a reason for learning the skill and describe how the skill relates to more advanced skills.

> *"The most difficult aspect of coaching is this: Coaches must learn to let athletes learn. Sport skills should be taught so they have meaning to the child, not just meaning to the coach."*
>
> Rainer Martens, ASEP Founder

Demonstrate the Skill

The demonstration step is the most important part of teaching sport skills to young players who may have never done anything closely resembling the skill. They need a picture, not just words. They need to see how the skill is performed.

If you are unable to perform the skill correctly, have an assistant coach, one of your players, or someone skilled in hockey perform the demonstration. These tips will help make your demonstrations more effective:

- Use correct form.
- Demonstrate the skill several times.
- Slow down the action, if possible, during one or two performances so players can see every movement involved in the skill.
- Perform the skill at different angles so your players can get a full perspective of it.
- Demonstrate the skill from both sides of the body and at each end of the rink.

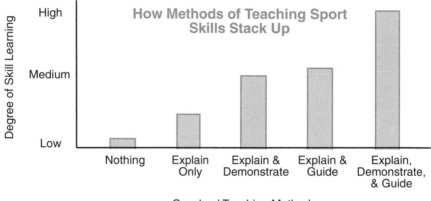

Explain the Skill

Players learn more effectively when they're given a brief explanation of the skill along with the demonstration. Use simple terms and, if possible, relate the skill to previously learned skills. Ask your players whether they understand your description. A good technique is to ask the team to repeat your explanation. Ask questions like "What are you going to do first?" "Then what?" Watch for looks of confusion or uncertainty and repeat your explanation and demonstration of those points. If possible, use different words so that your players get a chance to try to understand from a different perspective.

Complex skills often are better understood when they are explained in more manageable parts. For instance, if you want to teach your players how to change direction when they are skating with the puck/ball, you might take the following steps:

1. Show them a correct performance of the entire skill, and explain its function in hockey.
2. Break down the skill and point out its component parts to your players.
3. Have players perform each of the component skills you have already taught them, such as stick handling while skating forward or backward while keeping their head up, and pivoting front to back and back to front while skating with and without the puck/ball.
4. After players have demonstrated their ability to perform the separate parts of the skill in sequence, reexplain the entire skill.
5. Have players practice the skill.

One caution: Young players have short attention spans, and a long demonstration or explanation of the skill will bore them. So spend no more than a few minutes combined on the introduction, demonstration, and explanation phases. Then get the players active in attempts to perform the skill. The total IDEA should be completed in 10 minutes or less, followed by individual and group practice activities.

Attend to Players Practicing the Skill

If the skill you selected was within your players' capabilities, and you have done an effective job of introducing, demonstrating, and explaining it, your players should be ready to attempt the skill. Some players may need to be physically guided through the movements during their first few attempts. Walking unsure athletes through the skill in this way will help them gain confidence to perform the skill on their own.

Your teaching duties don't end when all your athletes have demonstrated that they understand how to perform the skill. In fact, a significant part of your teaching will involve observing closely the hit-and-miss trial performances of your players.

As you observe players' efforts in drills and activities, offer positive, corrective feedback in the form of the "compliment sandwich" described in unit 3. If a player performs the skill properly, acknowledge it and offer praise. Keep in mind that your feedback will have a great influence on your players' motivation to practice and improve their performance.

Remember, too, that young players need individual instruction. So set aside a time before, during, or after practice to give individual help.

What Planning Do I Need to Do?

Beginning coaches often make the mistake of showing up for the first practice with no particular plan in mind. These coaches find that their practices are unorganized, their players are frustrated and inattentive, and the amount and quality of their skill instruction is limited. Planning is essential to successful teaching and coaching. And it doesn't begin on the way to practice!

Preseason Planning

Effective coaches begin planning well before the start of the season. Among the preseason measures that will make the season more enjoyable, successful, and safe for you and your players are the following:

- Familiarize yourself with the sport organization you are involved in, especially its philosophy and goals regarding youth sport.
- Examine the availability of facilities, equipment, instructional aids, and other materials needed for practices and games.
- Find out what fund-raising you and your players will be expected to do, and decide on the best way to meet your goals.
- Make arrangements for any team travel that will be required during the season. Consider clearance forms, supervision, transportation, equipment, contacting parents, and safety.

- Check to see whether you have adequate liability insurance to cover you when one of your players is hurt (see unit 5). If you don't, get some.
- Establish your coaching priorities regarding having fun, developing players' skills, and winning.
- Select and meet with your assistant coaches to discuss the philosophy, goals, team rules, and plans for the season.
- Register players for the team. Have them complete a player information form and obtain medical clearance forms, if required.
- Institute an injury-prevention program for your players.
- Hold an orientation meeting to inform parents of your background, philosophy, goals, and instructional approach. Also,

give a brief overview of hockey rules, terms, and strategies to familiarize parents or guardians with the sport.

You may be surprised at the number of things you should do even before the first practice. But if you address them during the pre-season, the season will be much more enjoyable and productive for you and your players.

In-Season Planning

Your choice of activities during the season should be based on whether they will help your players develop physical and mental skills, knowledge of rules and game tactics, sportsmanship, and love for the sport. All of these goals are important, but we'll focus on the skills and tactics of hockey to give you an idea of how to itemize your objectives.

Goal Setting

What you plan to do during the season must be reasonable for the maturity and skill level of your players. In terms of hockey skills and tactics, you should teach young players the basics and move on to more complex activities only after the players have mastered these easier techniques and strategies.

To begin the season, your instructional goals might include the following:

- Players will be able to assume and maintain the ready position.
- Players will be able to perform stationary stick handling and stick handling with movement.
- Players will be able to make accurate forehand and backhand passes to stationary and moving teammates.
- Players will be able to give and accept passes while stationary or moving.
- Players will be able to take several different types of shots, especially a backhand, using correct shooting technique.
- Players will be able to move the puck/ball effectively into the offensive zone.
- Players will be able to transition quickly from offense to defense.
- Players will position themselves correctly in the defensive zone.
- Players will demonstrate knowledge of hockey rules and penalties.
- Players will demonstrate knowledge of basic offensive and defensive strategies.

Organizing

After you've defined the skills and tactics you want your players to learn during the season, you can plan how to teach them to your players in practices. But be flexible! If your players are having difficulty learning a skill or tactic, take some extra time until they get the hang of it—even if that means moving back your schedule. After all, if your players are unable to perform the fundamental skills, they'll never execute the more complex skills you have scheduled for them, and they won't have much fun trying.

Still, it helps to have a plan for progressing players through skills during the season. The 4-week sample season plan in Appendix B shows how to schedule your skill instruction in an organized and progressive manner. If this is your first coaching experience, you may wish to follow the plan as it stands. If you have some previous experience, you may want to modify the schedule to better fit the needs of your team.

The way you organize your season may also help your players to develop socially and psychologically. By giving your players responsibility for certain aspects of practices—leading warm-up and stretching activities are common examples—you help players to develop self-esteem and take responsibility for themselves and the team. As you plan your season, consider ways to provide your players with experiences that lead them to steadily improve these skills.

What Makes Up a Good Practice?

A good instructional plan makes practice preparation much easier. Have players work on more important and less difficult goals in early-season practice sessions. And see to it that players master basic skills before moving on to more advanced ones.

It is helpful to establish one goal for each practice; but try to include a variety of activities related to that goal. For example, although your primary objective might be to improve players' stick handling skills, you should have players perform several different drills designed to enhance that single skill. To add more variety to your practices, vary the order of the activities.

In general, we recommend that in each of your practices you do the following:

- *Warm up.*
- *Practice previously taught skills.*
- *Teach and practice new skills.*
- *Practice under competitive conditions.*
- *Cool down.*
- *Evaluate.*

Warm Up

As you're checking the roster and announcing the performance goals for the practice, your players should be preparing their bodies for vigorous activity. A 5- to 10-minute period of easy-paced activities, stretching, and calisthenics should be sufficient for youngsters to limb er their muscles and reduce the risk of injury. Because rink time is limited, have your players stretch off surface so you can maximize the time on the surface for teaching drills and game conditions.

Practice Previously Taught Skills

Devote part of each practice to having players work on the fundamental skills they already know. But remember, kids like variety. Thus you should organize and modify drills so that everyone is involved and stays interested. Praise and encourage players when you notice improvement, and offer individual assistance to those who need help.

Teach and Practice New Skills

Gradually build on your players' existing skills by giving players something new to practice each session. The proper method for teaching sport skills is described on pages 36–40. Refer to those pages if you have any questions about teaching new skills or if you want to evaluate your teaching approach periodically during the season.

Practice Under Competitive Conditions

Competition among teammates during practices prepares players for actual games and informs young athletes about their abilities relative to their peers. Youngsters also seem to have more fun in competitive activities.

You can create game-like conditions by using competitive drills, modified games, and scrimmages (see units 7 and 8). However, consider the following guidelines before introducing competition into your practices:

- All players should have an equal opportunity to participate.
- Match players by ability and physical maturity.
- Make sure that players can execute fundamental skills before they compete in groups.
- Emphasize performing well, not winning, in every competition.
- Give players room to make mistakes by avoiding constant evaluation of their performances.

Cool Down

Each practice should wind down with a 5- to 10-minute period of light exercise, including easy skating, performance of simple skills, and some stretching. The cool-down allows athletes' bodies to return to the resting state and avoid stiffness, and it affords you an opportunity to review the practice.

Evaluate

At the end of practice spend a few minutes with your players reviewing how well the session accomplished the goals you had set. Even if your evaluation is negative, show optimism for future practices and send players off on an upbeat note.

How Do I Put a Practice Together?

Simply knowing the six practice components is not enough. You must also be able to arrange those components into a logical progression and fit them into a time schedule. Now, using your instructional goals as a guide for selecting what skills to have your players work on, try to plan several hockey practices you might conduct. The following example should help you get started.

Sample Practice Plan

Performance Objective. Players will be able to give and accept passes on the forehand and backhand sides.

Component	Time	Activity or drill
Warm up	10 min	Stretching (off surface) Easy skating drills, using full surface length
Practice	20 min	Star Passing on the Circles Drill Two-On-Zero Passing Drill
Teach	15 min	Proper techniques of giving and accepting passes on the forehand and backhand sides
Scrimmage	15 min	Half surface, two-on-two, three-on-three scrimmage
Cool down and evaluate	10 min	Easy skating with or without the puck/ball Stretching (off surface)

✔ *Summary Checklist*

During your hockey season, check your planning and teaching skills periodically. As you gain more coaching experience, you should be able to answer "Yes" to each of the following.

When you plan, do you remember to plan for

____ preseason events such as player registration, fund-raising, travel, liability protection, use of facilities, and parent orientation?

____ season goals such as the development of players' physical skills, mental skills, sportsmanship, and enjoyment?

____ practice components such as warm-up, practicing previously taught skills, teaching and practicing new skills, practicing under game-like conditions, cool-down, and evaluation?

When you teach sport skills to your players, do you

____ arrange the players so all can see and hear?

____ introduce the skill clearly and explain its importance?

____ demonstrate the skill properly several times?

____ explain the skill simply and accurately?

____ attend closely to players practicing the skill?

____ offer corrective, positive feedback or praise after observing players' attempts at the skill?

Unit 5

What About Safety?

One of your players breaks free down the rink, skating toward the goal. But out of nowhere races a defender who catches up with and accidentally trips up the goal-bound player. You see that your player is not getting up from the ground and seems to be in pain. What do you do?

No coach wants to see players get hurt. But injury remains a reality of sport participation; consequently, you must be prepared to provide first aid when injuries occur and to protect yourself against unjustified lawsuits. Fortunately, there are many preventive measures coaches can institute to reduce the risk. This unit will describe how you can

- create the safest possible environment for your players,
- provide emergency first aid to players when they get hurt, and
- protect yourself from injury liability.

How Do I Keep My Players From Getting Hurt?

Injuries may occur because of poor preventive measures. Part of your planning, described in unit 4, should include steps that give your players the best possible chance for injury-free participation. These steps include the following:

- *Preseason physical examination*
- *Nutrition*
- *Physical conditioning*
- *Equipment and facilities inspection*
- *Matching athletes by physical maturity and warning of inherent risks*
- *Proper supervision and record keeping*

- *Providing water breaks*
- *Warm-up and cool-down*

Preseason Physical Examination

In the absence of severe injury or ongoing illness, your players should have a physical examination every 2 years. If a player has a known complication, a physician's consent should be obtained before participation is allowed. You should also have players' parents or guardians sign a participation agreement form and a release form to allow their children to be treated in the case of an emergency.

INFORMED CONSENT FORM

I hereby give my permission for _____ to participate

in _____ during the athletic season beginning in 199____. Further, I authorize the school to provide emergency treatment of an injury to or illness of my child if qualified medical personnel consider treatment necessary *and* perform the treatment. This authorization is granted only if I cannot be reached and a reasonable effort has been made to do so.

Date _____   Parent or guardian _____

Address _____   Phone ( ) _____

Family physician _____   Phone ( ) _____

Pre-existing medical conditions (e.g., allergies or chronic illnesses) _____

_____

Other(s) to also contact in case of emergency _____

Relationship to child _____   Phone ( ) _____

My child and I are aware that participating in _____ is a potentially hazardous activity. I assume all risks associated with participation in this sport, including but not limited to falls, contact with other participants, the effects of the weather, traffic, and other reasonable risk conditions associated with the sport. All such risks to my child are known and understood by me.

I understand this informed consent form and agree to its conditions on behalf of my child.

Child's signature _____   Date _____

Parent's signature _____   Date _____

Nutrition

Increasingly, disordered eating and unhealthy dietary habits are encroaching on youth hockey players. Let players and parents know the importance of healthy eating and the dangers that can arise from efforts to lose weight too quickly. Young hockey players need to supply their bodies with the extra energy they need to keep up with the demands of practices and games. Ask your director about information that you can pass on to your players and their parents, and include a discussion of basic, commonsense nutrition in your parent orientation meeting.

Physical Conditioning

Muscles, tendons, and ligaments unaccustomed to vigorous and long-lasting physical activity are prone to injury. Therefore, prepare your athletes to withstand the exertion of playing your sport. An effective conditioning program for hockey would involve running and other forms of aerobic activity.

Make conditioning drills and activities fun. Include a skill component, such as stick handling, to prevent players from becoming bored or looking upon the activity as work.

Keep in mind, too, that players on your team may respond differently to conditioning activities. Wide-ranging levels of fitness or natural ability might mean that an activity that challenges one child is beyond another's ability to complete safely. The environment is another factor that may affect players' responses to activity. The same workout that was effective in a cool ice rink might be hazardous to players on a hot, humid afternoon on the outside roller rink. Similarly, an activity children excel in at sea level might present a risk at higher altitudes. An ideal conditioning program prepares players for the season's demands without neglecting physical and environmental factors that affect their safety.

Equipment and Facilities Inspection

Another way to prevent injuries is to check the quality and fit of all of the protective equipment used by your players. Inspect the equipment before you distribute it, after you have assigned the equipment, and regularly during the season. Ensure that all players have adequate equipment that meets minimum requirements and suggest that they wear any recommended optional equipment. Worn-out, damaged, lost, or outdated equipment must be replaced immediately.

Remember, also, to examine regularly the rink on which your players practice and play. Remove hazards, report conditions you cannot remedy, and request maintenance as necessary. If unsafe conditions exist, either make adaptations to avoid risk to your players' safety or stop the practice or game until safe conditions have been restored.

Matching Athletes by Maturity and Warning of Inherent Risks

Children of the same age may differ in height and weight by up to 6 inches and 50 pounds. That's why in contact sports, or sports in which size provides an advantage, it's essential to match players against opponents of similar size and physical maturity. Such an approach gives smaller, less mature children a better chance to succeed and avoid injury, and provides larger children with more of a challenge.

Matching helps protect you from certain liability concerns. But you also must warn players of the inherent risks involved in playing hockey, because "failure to warn" is one of the most successful arguments in lawsuits against coaches. So, thoroughly explain the inherent risks of hockey, and make sure each player knows, understands, and appreciates those risks.

The preseason parent orientation meeting is a good opportunity to explain the risks of the sport to parents and players. It is also a good occasion on which to have both the players and their parents sign waivers releasing you from liability should an injury occur. (See a sample Informed Consent Form on page 51.) Such waivers do not relieve you of responsibility for your players' well-being, but they are recommended by lawyers.

Proper Supervision and Record Keeping

With youngsters, your mere presence in the area of play is not enough; you must actively plan and direct team activities and closely observe and evaluate players' participation. You're the watchdog responsible for the players' well-being. So if you notice a player limping or grimacing, give him or her a rest and examine the extent of the injury.

As a coach, you're also required to enforce the rules of the sport, prohibit dangerous horseplay, and hold practices only under safe weather conditions. These specific supervisory activities will make the play environment safer for your players and will help protect you from liability if a mishap does occur.

For further protection, keep records of your season plans, practice plans, and players' injuries. Season and practice plans come in handy when you need evidence that players have been taught certain skills, whereas accurate, detailed accident report forms offer protection against unfounded lawsuits. Ask for these forms from the organization to which you belong. And hold on to these records for several years so that an "old hockey injury" of a former player doesn't come back to haunt you.

Providing Water Breaks

Encourage players to drink plenty of water before, during, and after practice. Because water makes up 45% to 65% of a youngster's body weight and water weighs about a pound per pint, the loss of even a little bit of water can have severe consequences for the body's systems. Players can become dehydrated even though they are skating on a cool ice rink. Nor do players have to feel thirsty; in fact, by the time they are aware of their thirst, they are long overdue for a drink.

Warm-Up and Cool-Down

Although young bodies are generally very limber, they, too, can get tight from inactivity. Therefore, a warm-up period of approximately 10 minutes before each practice is strongly recommended. Warm-up should address each muscle group and get the heart rate elevated in preparation for strenuous activity. Easy skating followed by stretching activities is a common sequence.

As practice is winding down, slow players' heart rates with easy skating or other light activity. Then arrange for a 5- to 10-minute period of easy stretching at the end of practice to help players avoid stiff muscles and make them less tight before the next practice.

What if One of My Players Gets Hurt?

No matter how good and thorough your prevention program, injuries will occur. When injury does strike, chances are you will be the one in charge. The severity and nature of the injury will determine how actively involved you'll be in treating the injury. But regardless of how seriously a player is hurt, it is your responsibility to know what steps to take. So let's look at how you can provide basic emergency care to your injured athletes.

Minor Injuries

Although no injury seems minor to the person experiencing it, most injuries are neither life-threatening nor severe enough to restrict participation. When such injuries occur, you can take an active role in their initial treatment.

ASEP Fact

You shouldn't let a fear of acquired immune deficiency syndrome (AIDS) stop you from helping a player. On the rink you are only at risk if you allow contaminated blood to come in contact with an open wound, so the blood barrier that you wear will protect you from AIDS should one of your players carry this disease. Check with your director or ASEP for more information about protecting yourself and your participants from AIDS.

Scrapes and Cuts

When one of your players has an open wound, the first thing you should do is to put on a pair of disposable surgical gloves or some other effective blood barrier. Then follow these four steps:

1. Stop the bleeding by applying direct pressure with a clean dressing to the wound and elevating it. The player may be able to apply this pressure while you put on your gloves. Do not remove the dressing if it becomes soaked with blood. Instead, place an additional dressing on top of the one already in place. If bleeding continues, elevate the injured area above the heart and maintain pressure.

2. Cleanse the wound thoroughly once the bleeding is controlled. A good rinsing with a forceful stream of water, and perhaps light scrubbing with soap, will help prevent infection.

3. Protect the wound with sterile gauze or a bandage. If the player continues to participate, apply protective padding over the injured area.

4. <u>Remove and dispose of gloves</u> carefully to prevent you or anyone else from coming into contact with blood.

For bloody noses not associated with serious facial injury, have the athlete sit and lean slightly forward. Then pinch the player's nostrils shut. If the bleeding continues after several minutes, or if the athlete has a history of nosebleeds, seek medical assistance.

Strains and Sprains

The physical demands of hockey practices and games often result in injury to the muscles or tendons (strains), or to the ligaments (sprains). When your players suffer minor strains or sprains, immediately apply the PRICE method of injury care.

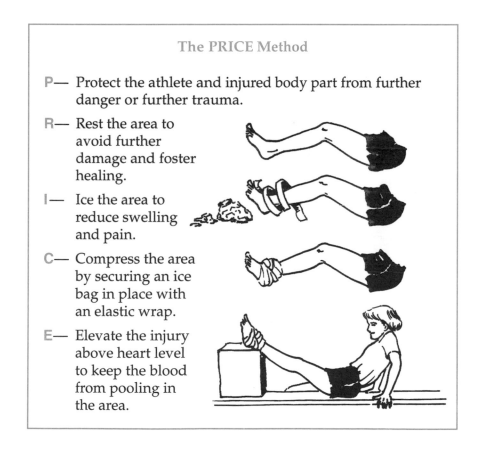

The PRICE Method

P— Protect the athlete and injured body part from further danger or further trauma.

R— Rest the area to avoid further damage and foster healing.

I— Ice the area to reduce swelling and pain.

C— Compress the area by securing an ice bag in place with an elastic wrap.

E— Elevate the injury above heart level to keep the blood from pooling in the area.

Bumps and Bruises

Inevitably, hockey players make contact with each other and with the surface or rink. If the force of a body part at impact is great enough, a bump or bruise will result. Many players continue playing with such sore spots, but if the bump or bruise is large and painful, you should act appropriately. Enact the PRICE method of injury care and monitor the injury. If swelling, discoloration, and pain have lessened, the player may resume participation with protective padding; if not, the player should be examined by a physician.

Serious Injuries

Head, neck, and back injuries; fractures; and injuries that cause a player to lose consciousness are among a class of injuries that you cannot and should not try to treat yourself. But you should plan for what you'll do if such an injury occurs. And your plan should include the following guidelines for action:

- Obtain the phone number and ensure the availability of nearby emergency care units. Include this information as part of a written emergency plan before the season, and have it with you at every practice and match.
- Assign an assistant coach or another adult the responsibility of knowing the location of the nearest phone and contacting emergency medical help upon your request.
- Ensure that emergency medical information, treatment, and transportation consent forms are available during every practice and match.
- Do not move the injured athlete.
- Calm the injured athlete and keep others away from him or her as much as possible.
- Evaluate whether the athlete's breathing is stopped or irregular, and if necessary, clear the airway with your fingers.
- Administer artificial respiration if breathing is stopped. Administer cardiopulmonary resuscitation (CPR), or have a trained individual administer CPR, if the athlete's circulation has stopped.
- Remain with the athlete until medical personnel arrive.

How Do I Protect Myself?

When one of your players is injured, naturally your first concern is his or her well-being. Your feelings for children, after all, are what made you decide to coach. Unfortunately, there is something else that you must consider: Can you be held liable for the injury?

From a legal standpoint, a coach has nine duties to fulfill. We've discussed all but planning (see unit 4) in this unit:

1. Provide a safe environment.
2. Properly plan the activity.
3. Provide adequate and proper equipment.
4. Match or equate athletes.
5. Warn of inherent risks in the sport.
6. Supervise the activity closely.
7. Evaluate athletes for injury or incapacitation.
8. Know emergency procedures and first aid.
9. Keep adequate records.

In addition to fulfilling these nine legal duties, you should check your insurance coverage to make sure your policy will protect you from liability.

Summary Self-Test

Now that you've read how to make your coaching experience safe for your players and yourself, test your knowledge of the material by answering these questions:

1. What are eight injury-prevention measures you can institute to try to keep your players from getting hurt?

2. What is the four-step emergency care process for cuts?

3. What method of treatment is best for minor sprains and strains?

4. What steps can you take to manage serious injuries?

5. What are the nine legal duties of a coach?

Unit 6

What Is Hockey All About?

Chances are you've witnessed or even experienced personally the excitement of a hockey game. You know the thrill of threading the puck/ball up the surface with crisp, clean passes, dodging defenders, and then finishing the end-to-end run with a snappy wrist shot that the goalkeeper turns away with a great kick save. Rushing back to play defense, your legs feel a little rubbery and you're breathing hard, but all you can think about is how good it felt to skate so fast. Whether it's a 7-year-old in his or her first game or a 20-year-old in a collegiate playoff, the thrill is there for everyone.

As a hockey coach, you will have the fun of introducing kids to this exciting sport. Reading the first part of this book will give you a good overview of what it takes to be a coach. The next three units of *Coaching Youth Hockey* provide the ice and roller hockey basics: the rules, skills, tactics, and drills you and your hockey players should know.

Coaching Hockey: Worth a Shot

Hockey is exciting, fast growing, and, most of all, a fun game to play. Hockey comes from Canada and is thought to be its national sport (actually lacrosse is Canada's national sport). Hockey's popularity has increased recently, and more children are expressing an interest in playing some form of the game. This book refers to two forms of hockey. One is traditional, *ice hockey*, and the other is the newcomer, *roller hockey*, or *in-line hockey*. We prefer to use the term *roller hockey* because of the roots of the sport. Roller hockey was developed and is still played today in New York, using the traditional quad or four-wheel skate, but today the in-line skate is more popular.

Throughout the United States, youth ice hockey is governed by USA Hockey, from the mite division (9-year-olds and under) to the U.S. Olympic team. USA Hockey is responsible for team insurance, rules, training of both players and officials, and quality control of the amateur game. On a professional level, the National Hockey League (NHL) reaches out to ice hockey players in North America and Europe. The NHL can be seen in most major markets in North America, and some of its members are excellent role models for young athletes. The NHL, which is closely involved with youth programs throughout North America, readily assists new coaches.

The United States Amateur Confederation of Roller Skating (USAC/RS) is the Olympic national governing body for roller hockey. The USAC/RS governs a number of leagues from local recreational leagues to Olympic and other international competitions. Like USA Hockey, USAC/RS provides insurance and rules, training for players, coaches, and officials, and quality control for amateur competition. The National In-Line Hockey Association (NIHA) also plays a leading role in roller hockey in the United States. NIHA offers league and team memberships, as well as help in establishing new leagues and provides insurance and rules for teams. USA Hockey has also established a new subdivision within its organization for roller hockey. See your sport director to ensure that you know which organization's guidelines you should follow.

Increasing popularity of roller hockey has resulted in a new professional league called Roller Hockey International (RHI). Most RHI players are minor league ice hockey players, but numbers of full-time roller hockey players are rising. The RHI's inaugural season included 12 teams, but the increasing number of teams seen in most major markets and on television coverage by ESPN suggest that RHI will continue to grow and provide additional opportunities for young roller hockey players.

Approaches to Hockey

Most 5- to 6-year-old girls and boys are developmentally ready to play competitive ice and roller hockey. Noncompetitive players sometimes begin as early as ages 3 to 4 for roller hockey and 4 to 5 for ice hockey. Hockey requires children to develop their skating skills, and players must skate well enough to be able to focus on other aspects of the game.

The skating ability of beginning roller hockey players is generally slightly more advanced than that of beginning ice hockey players. Roller hockey players can practice on the driveway, street, or basement floor, but ice hockey players must either wait for freezing temperatures or for someone to take them to an ice rink. Table 6.1 shows other major differences between the two sports. Four-on-four play, no offsides, no neutral zone, no clearing (icing), and a concentration on offense are some of the differences that allow roller hockey to be a wide open, high-scoring game.

Table 6.1 Differences Between Ice and Roller Hockey		
Category	**Ice hockey**	**Roller hockey**
Number of players playing at one time/ team	Five plus a goalie	13 years old and under–five plus a goalie 13 years old and over– four plus a goalie
Object played with	Standard size and weight puck	A ball or several different types of pucks
Offside lines	Blue line	Center line or blue line or no offside
Sending the puck/ball the length of the surface	Icing	Clearing
Goal dimensions	Standard 4' × 6'	4' × 6' for tournaments or alternate size for leagues
Rink markings	See Figure 6.1	See Figure 6.2
Rink sizes	Min. 185' × 85' Max. 200' × 100'	Min. 145' × 65' Max. 200' × 100'
Number of periods	Three	Two, three, or four

Age Guidelines

USA Hockey has established the following age classifications for all *ice hockey* teams playing under its rules:

	Boys	Girls
Mites	9 or younger	
Squirts	10–13	8–12
Peewees	12–13	13–15
Bantams	14–15	
Midgets	16–17	16–19

Note. Girls playing on boys' teams must conform to boys' age classifications.

Roller hockey age divisions vary significantly from league to league. USAC/RS Puck Hockey players fall under one of four categories: Senior, 18 years and older; Junior, 15–17; Bantam, 12–14; Peewee, 11 and younger (only allowed at the state level). USAC/RS North American-Style Ball Hockey players are classified as Senior if 16 years and older or Junior if 12–16 years (16-year-olds might play as Juniors if they were 15 on January 1 of the competitive year). Finally, USA Roller Hockey, another USAC/RS league, offers a Senior division for players 13 and older and a Junior division for players 6–12. NIHA has established these age classifications for its teams (boys and girls play under the same age classifications): 7 years or younger, 8–9, 10–11, 12–13, 14–15. High school ages are grouped together.

What Are the Rules?

Like any other game, hockey needs rules to keep the game safe. Unfortunately, ice hockey rules have become a bit confusing, and in roller hockey the "rules" are more like a set of guidelines. The best way to understand the rules fully is to take a referee class, which not only helps you keep up with the rules, but also to understand what officials go through during a game.

Rink Dimensions

Rink dimensions vary so widely that it is impossible to list every option. Roller hockey rinks vary even more than their ice hockey counterparts. We have tried to list minimum and maximum sizes for ice and roller hockey rinks. If you have any questions about requirements for your rink, call the appropriate governing body (USA Hockey, USAC/RS, or NIHA).

Ice Hockey

Ice hockey is played on an ice surface known as a rink. Generally, the rink should be 200 feet long and 100 feet wide. Variations in the size rink you are playing on usually are fine unless you want to host a major tournament or game; then the dimensions cannot be less than 185 feet long by 85 feet wide. The rink is surrounded by a wooden or fiberglass wall or fence known as the *boards*. The boards are at least 40 inches but not more than 48 inches high (the ideal height is 42 inches).

The rink is divided into three parts: two blue lines and one red line. The blue lines divide the surface into offensive and defensive portions. The red line divides the surface into two equal parts and is used to determine *icing*, which is a stoppage of play that occurs when a team sends the puck down the length of the ice from its side of the red line. The neutral zone is the area between the two blue lines that includes the center line.

There are two goals, located a minimum of 12 feet to a maximum of 15 feet from each end of the rink. Each goal must be 4 feet wide and 6 feet high and include a net attached to the frame so a puck shot into the net cannot pass through it. A goal line should be drawn across the opening of the goal and continue across the surface extending from each goal post. For a goal to be scored, the puck must cross over the goal line *completely*. The face-off spots, circles, and goal creases are identified in Figure 6.1.

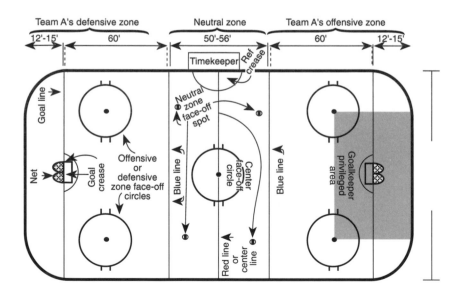

■ **Figure 6.1**   Ice hockey rink.

Roller Hockey

Roller hockey is also played on a rink, either outdoors or enclosed within an indoor facility. The dimensions are typically 180 feet long and 80 feet wide. The rules allow surfaces ranging from as large as 200 feet long by 100 feet wide to 145 feet long by 65 feet wide. The rink is surrounded by a bordering material known as the *structure*, which extends neither less than 8 inches nor more than 48 inches above the playing surface.

The rink is divided into two halves by a center line that is 12 inches wide. The center line itself is considered a neutral area. A team's goal area is called the *defending zone*, and the opposing team's area is called the *attacking zone*.

The official size of the goal net is 4 feet wide and 6 feet high. Alternative sizes are acceptable for regular league play, but official-sized goals must be used for all tournament and championship play. A net should be attached to the goal so a puck/ball shot into the net cannot pass through it. The goals should be placed 10 to 15 feet from the end of the rink. A goal line should be drawn across the opening of the goal and continue across the surface extending from each goal post. To score a goal, the puck/ball must cross over the goal line *completely*. The face-off spots, circles, and goal creases are identified in Figure 6.2.

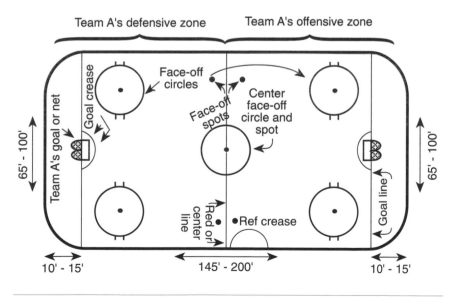

Figure 6.2 Roller hockey rink.

Player Equipment

Both ice and roller hockey players may try to modify equipment to enhance their play, such as adjusting the curvature of a stick. Although explicit rules determine how curved a stick can be, players will try to use a little extra curvature to help their game. As coach, you must be responsible for your players and ensure that they play within the equipment guidelines established by your league or governing body.

It is important for new coaches and parents to understand the importance of proper fitting gear. Ill-fitting equipment can hinder the movements of the player, thereby creating a safety hazard as well as decreasing the player's enjoyment of the sport.

Ice Hockey

In ice hockey, the shaft of the stick should not exceed 60 inches in length, and the blade should be no more than 12½ inches long. The width of the blade should be neither more than 3 inches nor less than 2 inches at any point. Curvature is generally restricted to ½ inch, but restrictions may vary among leagues. Check with your league administrator for rules applying to your team. The blade of the goalkeeper's stick should not be more than 3½ inches wide at any point except the heel, where it must not exceed 4½ inches. The blade cannot exceed 15½ inches from the heel to the end of the blade. The widened portion of the goalkeeper's stick, extending up the shaft, can neither extend beyond 26 inches in length nor 3½ inches in width.

At a very early age players learn to change the curve on their sticks. They believe that the more the stick is curved the easier it is to lift the puck off the surface. This is not entirely true as the follow-through of the pass or shot will cause the puck to rise. Another factor leading players to curve their sticks illegally is the old street hockey sticks with plastic blades. Directions on the package teach youngsters how to heat the blade (with parental supervision) to bend it into any curve players want. There are no referees in street hockey, so the *banana hook* has become a favorite. Unfortunately, this practice has been brought into both ice and roller hockey. Coaches beware.

All skates and skate blades should be approved for ice hockey by the Hockey Equipment Certification Council (HECC), an independent organization responsible for the development, evaluation, and testing of ice hockey equipment. To date, standards exist for face masks, helmets, and skate blades.

All players are also required to wear an HECC-approved helmet and face mask, hockey gloves, elbow protection, a hockey pant or hip protection, shin pads (non-goalkeepers) and goal pads (goalkeepers), athletic support and cup (males). Players are also highly encouraged to wear shoulder pads. Goalkeepers must wear chest and arm protectors. All players, including the goalkeeper, in the Peewee through Junior and all girls and women age classifications are required to wear an internal mouthguard, which covers all the teeth of one jaw, customarily the upper. Figure 6.3 (see page 70) illustrates standard ice and roller hockey equipment.

Roller Hockey

Roller hockey stick dimensions are the same as ice hockey, except that USAC/RS allows goalkeepers' sticks to be somewhat wider, not to exceed 5 inches at any point except the heel, where 5½ inches is the limit. USAC/RS and NIHA require roller hockey players to wear the following equipment (see Figure 6.3): head protection (hockey helmet with chin straps), face protection (full face cage or full face shield), mouthguard, elbow pads, hand protection (hockey gloves), knee and shin protection, and a jock strap and protective cup (males). In addition, USAC/RS requires all eyeglass wearers to use plastic lenses; glass lenses are prohibited. USAC/RS Puck Hockey and North American-Style Ball Hockey goalkeepers must wear full head protection masks, and all other equipment must be designed for head or body protection and may not give goalies an unfair advantage. USA Roller Hockey goalkeepers must wear leg guards, face mask, gloves, chest protector, goalkeeper's gloves, and goalkeeper's pads. Because specific requirements may vary, check with your director to ensure that your players' equipment meets league standards.

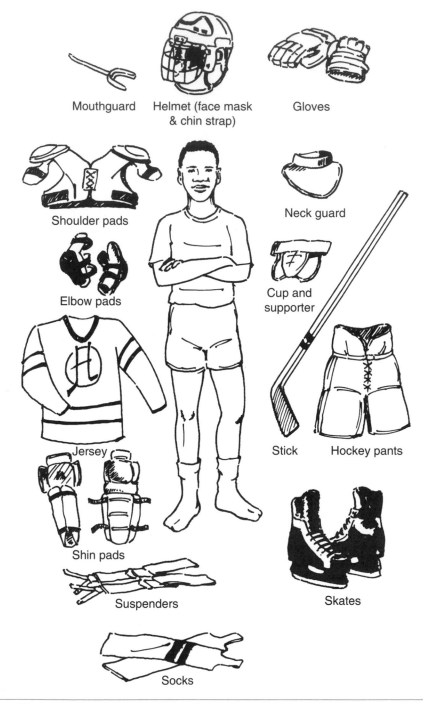

Mouthguard Helmet (face mask & chin strap) Gloves

Shoulder pads

Neck guard

Elbow pads

Cup and supporter

Jersey

Stick Hockey pants

Shin pads

Suspenders

Skates

Socks

■ **Figure 6.3**   Ice and roller hockey equipment.

Table 6.2 lists equipment required for ice and roller hockey.

Table 6.2 Ice and Roller Hockey Equipment		
Equipment	Ice hockey	Roller hockey
Helmet and face mask	Yes	Yes
Chin strap	Yes	Yes
Mouthguard	Yes	Yes
Elbow pads	Yes	Yes
Skates	Yes	Yes
Stick	Yes	Yes
Jersey	Yes	Yes
Shin pads	Yes	Yes
Gloves	Yes	Yes
Shoulder pads	Yes	Optional
Hockey pants or hip pads	Yes	Yes
Suspenders	Optional	Optional
Socks	Optional	Optional
Neck guards	Optional	Optional
Cup and supporter	Yes (males)	Yes (males)

Player Positions

One of the hardest concepts for coaches to teach players, especially beginners, is that everyone cannot merely skate around and chase the puck/ball. The best way to teach a team a positional plan is to teach all positions to all players. This approach will take some time, but the rewards will be well worth it. Don't forget to use the classroom to start this process. A classroom, chalk board, and the Xs and Os are some of your best coaching tools!

Ice Hockey

Each team fields five players plus a goalkeeper. Traditionally, there is one center, a left wing, a right wing, a left defensive player, and a right defensive player. Figure 6.4 illustrates the standard opening face-off. The center has the responsibility to take most of the face-offs and be the quarterback, while the wingers

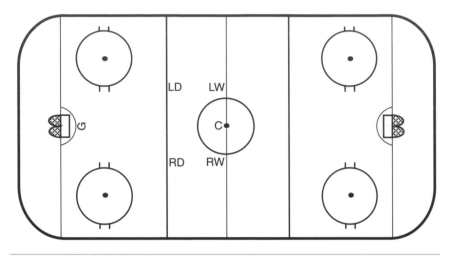

■ **Figure 6.4** Ice hockey (five-on-five) opening face-off.

support the center and help move the puck down the ice. Figure 6.5 shows the offensive lanes that the center and wings are responsible for while on offense. On defense the center's responsibility is helping defend in front of the net. The wingers skate in their lanes (see Figure 6.6) back-checking in the neutral and offensive zones. When they enter the defensive zone, they cover the opposing defensive players up high (near the blue line). On

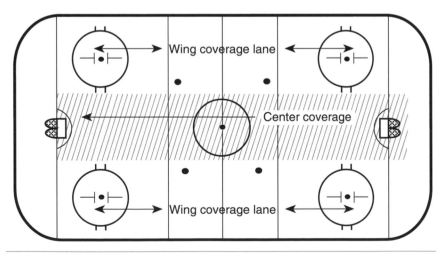

■ **Figure 6.5** Ice hockey offensive lane coverage for forwards.

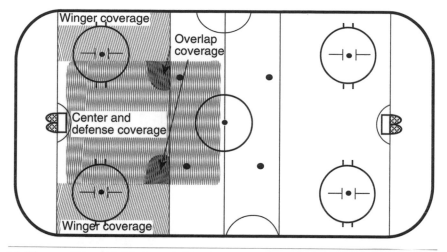

■ **Figure 6.6** Ice hockey defensive lane coverage for forwards.

offense, the defensive players initiate the breakout of the defensive zone and stay just inside the blue line in the offensive zone (see Figure 6.7). On defense, the defensive players go into the corners and cover the opposition in front of the net (see Figure 6.8). Some coaches teach that no one ever chases the opposition behind its own net. Instead the team defends in front of it and watches for a pass out in front of the net.

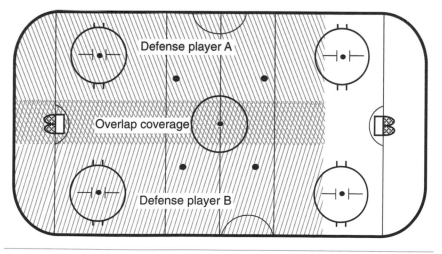

■ **Figure 6.7** Ice hockey offensive lane coverage for defensive players.

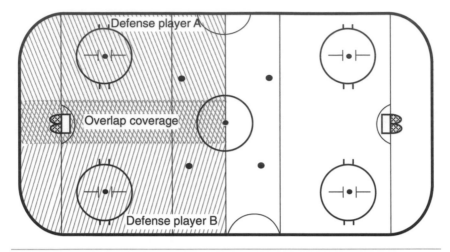

■ Figure 6.8 Ice hockey defensive lane coverage for defensive players.

Roller Hockey

Each team fields either four or five players plus a goalkeeper. If the age division fields five skaters, the previous ice hockey formations and responsibilities are the same for roller hockey. When a team fields four skaters, however, the traditional ice hockey formation no longer fits. The standard four-on-four formation of players includes one center, a left and right wing, and a defensive player. Figure 6.9 illustrates the standard opening face-off. The offensive responsibilities of the players do not change from the previously mentioned ice hockey positions. The defensive responsibilities change due to the lack of the second defensive player. Therefore, most teams have the second player back (no matter who it is) become the second defensive player, and then the center and the other player cover the opposition's defensive player up high. The defensive player's and center's responsibilities do not change from the previously described ice hockey coverage.

Goalkeepers in both ice and roller hockey are not restricted to staying in the net, but they also are not allowed to play beyond the offensive side of the red line. Most goalkeepers stay in their crease where they are allowed to fall on or freeze the puck/ball. Goalkeepers are the only players allowed to cover the puck/ball with their hands.

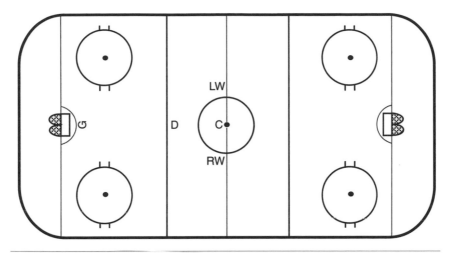

■ **Figure 6.9**   Roller hockey (four-on-four) opening face-off.

Officials

In both ice and roller hockey leagues, games are regulated by referees or linespeople whose main objective is to maintain control of the game and the players. They should maintain a safety-first attitude and act in a professional manner. All decisions made by referees are final.

Depending on the level of play, the number of referees and linespeople may vary, so do not be surprised if you have only one referee to officiate your games. It is important that all referees and linespeople have some type of training, which they usually obtain by attending a certified referee clinic given by USA Hockey or NIHA, or through USAC/RS's certification program. All referees should operate under official rules governing the league. The officials should be on the surface before the teams enter and remain until all players have left the surface. Remember that the referees' presence does not alleviate your responsibility as a coach for maintaining the conduct of your team. Also keep in mind that an official may issue a penalty even after a game has ended.

Length of the Game

Ice and roller hockey differ in the amount of game time allotted. Usually the determining factor is the rink schedule. If the rink is dedicated to other activities (e.g., public skating), as so many are, then the total time needed to complete the game is more important than the game-playing time. For instance, if a team receives 1 hour to play a game, the rink will probably be available only for 1 hour. Typically, youth ice hockey games require 1½ hours, and roller hockey games require 1 hour of available rink time.

Ice hockey rules establish the regulation time for a game as three 20-minute periods of play with a rest intermission between periods. Most ice hockey games are played with a stop-time clock: At every whistle the clock stops, and when the puck is dropped, the clock resumes. For younger players, a running-time clock is acceptable. The clock only stops for time-outs, injury, or rink repair. Generally, determine the actual time needed to complete a stop-time game by doubling the stop time. For example, if you were playing 15-minute periods in stop time, then you would need 90 minutes to complete a game (15 min/period × 3 = 45 min actual playing time × 2 = 90 min), with minimal rest intervals between periods. Each team is allowed a single 1-minute time-out per game. If a team requests an additional time-out, a minor penalty for delay of game is assessed.

Some roller hockey leagues have adopted the ice hockey format explained previously. USAC/RS recommends playing games in two 15-minute periods with a 3-minute rest in between and requires this format for North American-Style Ball Hockey championship games. USAC/RS Puck Hockey championships follow the same two-period format and rest time, but periods may be 10, 12, or 15 minutes long. NIHA suggests that the maximum time allotted for a game be 1 hour from the time a team enters the rink surface to the conclusion of the game. The game should be made up of two equal halves broken down as follow:

1. A 5-minute warm-up period before the beginning of the game; and

2. Two 22-minute running-time halves, with a 5-minute rest period between the halves, or two 12- to 15-minute stop-time halves, with a 5-minute rest period between halves.

Each team is allowed a single 1-minute time-out per game. Again, if a team requests an additional time-out, a minor penalty for the delay of game is assessed to that team.

Tied games in both ice and roller hockey remain tied at the end of regulation play, are extended for one period of sudden death play (variable lengths of time—usually 5 minutes), or are determined by a shoot-out. In a shoot-out, a predetermined number of players from each team goes in on the goalkeeper one-on-one until there is a goal advantage for one team. This is probably the most exciting way to end a game from a fan's point of view, but from a hockey purist's view, not the fairest. The hockey purist would prefer to see the game end in a tie or to play a full overtime period to decide the game's outcome.

Beginning Play

In ice and roller hockey, the game begins with a center face-off, and each period or half is started in similar fashion. A center face-off is also held after each goal is scored. A *face-off* is the action of the referee dropping the puck/ball between the sticks of two opposing players to start or resume play. Players facing off must stand facing opposite ends of the rink (toward the opposition's goalkeeper), approximately one stick length apart, with the blades of their sticks touching the surface of the rink. No other players should be allowed within the face-off circle until the puck/ball has been dropped by the referee. Once the puck/ball is dropped, the clock resumes (if playing with a stop-time clock).

Stoppages of Play

A stoppage of play results when a referee or linesperson blows the whistle for whatever reason. At no other time, except when a goal is scored, do players stop playing without the sound of a referee's whistle (USA Hockey occasionally changes this rule—some years a whistle is blown for a goal and some years it is not—be aware of your local rules). Some of the reasons why a referee would blow the whistle are

- player in the opposing team's crease (if not pushed or held there by an opposing player);
- puck/ball shot out of the rink;
- penalty called by an official;
- end of the period;
- puck/ball covered by the goalkeeper;
- puck/ball lodged on the back or top of the net;
- puck/ball lodged in someone's clothing; and
- offsides and icing (clearing in roller hockey).

For a beginning coach it is not essential to know where the face-offs for stoppages occur, but you should know that there are offensive and defensive face-offs, each of which is important for different reasons. The offensive face-off is important because it is the only time you can stop and position your players for an advantage. Figures 6.10a-b show two different offensive face-off positions each for ice and roller hockey. Try to figure out what is happening and position your players to get the best offensive opportunity. The defensive face-off is also very important because it is the only time that you can place your defense in a position to match the opposition. You should teach your centers or other face-off people not to rush into the face-off circle but to look around to make sure everyone is in the proper position. See Figures 6.11a-b for two different defensive face-off positions each for ice and roller hockey. The referee cannot drop the puck/ball until the centers or face-off people are in position. Face-offs will be further discussed in unit 7.

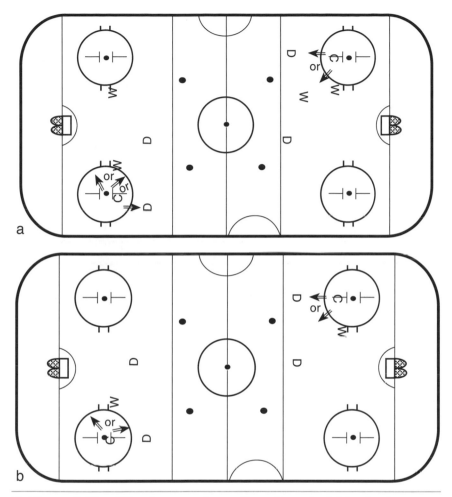

■ **Figure 6.10** Offensive zone face-off positions for (a) ice hockey (five-on-five) and (b) roller hockey (four-on-four).

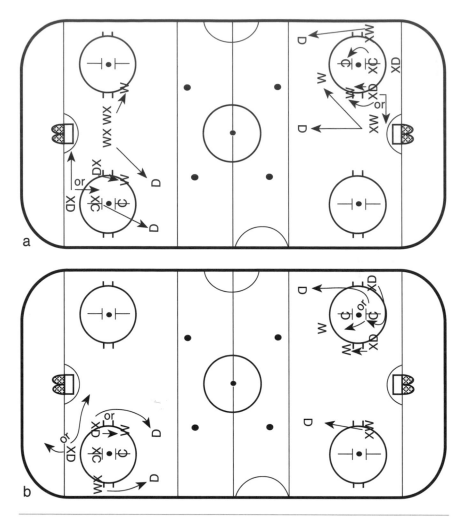

■ **Figure 6.11** Defensive zone face-off positions for (a) ice hockey
(five-on-five) and (b) roller hockey (four-on-four).

Penalties

A *penalty* is any infraction of the rules that govern play. If the team
in possession of the puck/ball commits an infraction, the referee
will immediately blow the whistle, stop play, and assess a penalty. If
an infraction is committed by the team not in possession of the puck/
ball, a delayed penalty will be signaled. At this time, the team in
possession of the puck/ball can substitute a player for its goalkeeper.

The goalkeeper skates to the bench, and the substitute is allowed to join play as a regular player.

Beginning coaches need not worry that the opposition will score by leaving the net unattended in a delayed penalty situation. Once the puck/ball is controlled by the team causing the infraction, the referee will immediately blow the whistle, stop play, and assess the penalty. There is always a chance of scoring on your own net, but this does not occur very often.

Penalties are grouped into six categories. Some infractions may have several different assessments, depending on the severity, intent, and discretion of the referee. Most ice and roller hockey penalties are similar. Table 6.3 illustrates the most common penalties for ice and roller hockey. See Appendix C on page 171 for illustrations of the referee signals that correspond to each penalty.

If a goalkeeper is assessed a minor penalty, a substitute player who was on the surface at that time will be allowed to serve the penalty for the goalkeeper, and the offending team will skate a player down. If a goal is scored by the opposing team while the offending team is skating a player down for a minor penalty (which is a *power-play goal*), the offending player's penalty is over once the goal is scored, and that player is allowed to re-enter play. During a major penalty, the player must serve the entire 5 minutes of the penalty, even if the opposing team scores a goal. For a second major penalty assessed to a player in a single game (goalkeeper included), a game misconduct penalty will be assessed in addition to the major penalty. That player will be suspended from play for the remainder of the game.

At the discretion of the referee, any infraction that would normally be a minor penalty can also be upgraded to a major penalty, depending on the severity and intent of the penalty. Any minor penalty infraction that causes an opponent to bleed results in the player being given a game misconduct penalty. After a misconduct penalty has expired, the player may not return to the game until there is a stoppage of play. A player who is assessed a misconduct penalty along with another penalty will serve the penalties back to back. If a substitute player is needed, that player must serve the original penalties plus all misconduct penalties. A suspension can be assessed for deliberately attempting to injure a player—which includes fighting, slashing, spearing, intentional tripping, kicking a player, and so on. Kicking a player may also lead to an automatic suspension, subject to review by the governing body of your league or organization.

Table 6.3 Ice and Roller Hockey Penalties		
Type of penalty	**Penalties for ice**	**Penalties for roller**
Minor penalties Generally: Ice = 2-min penalty Roller = 2- or 3-min penalty: 2 min for stop time and 3 min for running time	Holding, hooking, interference, tripping, delay of game, high-sticking, charging, slashing, elbowing, roughing, cross-checking, grasping the face mask, checking from behind, playing with illegal equipment, and abusing official	Holding, hooking, interference, tripping, delay of game, high-sticking, checking, slashing, elbowing, roughing, cross-checking, playing with illegal equipment, and abusing official
Major penalties Some major penalties come with a miscon-duct or game miscon-duct. Generally: Ice = 5-min penalty Roller = 5-min penalty plus in some instances a penalty shot	Cross-checking, boarding, elbowing, kneeing, slashing, checking after a whistle, checking from behind, fighting, spearing, butt-ending, attempting to injure	Cross-checking, boarding, elbowing, kneeing, slashing, checking after a whistle, grasping the face mask, checking from behind, fighting, spearing, butt-ending, attempting to injure, and boarding
Misconduct There are several types of misconduct: **General misconduct** = removal of player for 10 min without making team short-handed **Game misconduct** = suspension of player for rest of that game without making team shorthanded **Gross misconduct** = su pension of player for the rest of that game without making	Most of the major penalties above come with a misconduct or game misconduct, also: not surrendering a stick for measurement, abusing official, mouthguard violation, leaving bench during an altercation, and striking, attempting to injure, touching, or holding a game official.	Most of the major penalties above come with a misconduct or game misconduct, also: not surrendering a stick for measurement; abusing official; mouthguard violation; leaving bench during an altercation; and striking, attempting to injure, touching, or holding a game official.

Table 6.3 *(continued)*

team shorthanded with the possibility of further suspension of that player from the league

Match penalties
Suspension of player for the rest of that game without making team shorthanded with further suspension of that player from the league

Attempting to injure opponent, deliberately injuring opponent, swinging stick at opponent, and taped hand cutting opponent in altercation

Attempting to injure opponent, deliberately injuring opponent, swinging stick at opponent, and taped hand cutting opponent in altercation

Penalty shot
A goal instead of a penalty shot can be awarded if in the eyes of the official the puck/ball would have gone into the net.

Deliberate illegal substitution, goalkeeper deliberately displaces goal (non-breakaway), deliberate removal of goalkeeper's helmet/facemask, player falling on puck in crease, picking up puck in crease, throwing stick at puck in defensive end, and illegal entry into game on a breakaway

Deliberate illegal substitution, goalkeeper deliberately displaces goal (non-breakaway), deliberate removal of goalkeeper's helmet/facemask, player falling on puck/ball in crease, picking up puck/ball in crease, throwing stick at puck/ball in defensive end, and illegal entry into game on a breakaway

Goalkeeper's penalties
Besides the regular minor penalties, a goalkeeper can receive a minor penalty for these infractions.

Wearing or playing with illegal equipment, leaving crease during an altercation, participating in play across center line, going to bench for a stick during a stoppage, piling up obstacles in front of goal cage, holding puck more than 3 seconds after warning from official, and shooting puck directly out of play

Wearing or playing with illegal equipment, leaving crease during an altercation, participating in play across center line, going to bench for stick during a stoppage, piling up obstacles in front of goal cage, holding puck/ball more than 3 seconds after warning from official, and shooting puck/ball directly out of play

A penalty shot may result from a number of infractions, ranging from interference on a breakaway to illegal substitution. Check your league rules for a complete list of these infractions. During a penalty shot, the referee will signal play to begin by blowing a whistle. The player taking the penalty shot must maintain a forward motion at all times, and no goal will be allowed to score from a rebound. The goalkeeper must remain in contact with the crease area until the player taking the penalty shot makes contact with the puck/ball. If the goalkeeper leaves the crease prematurely, the referee may give the player a second chance. If no goal is scored, there will be a face-off in the nearest face-off spot in the defensive zone of the offending team. If the infraction that caused a penalty shot was minor, the team committing the penalty will not skate a player down when play resumes, regardless of whether a goal is scored on the penalty shot. Major, match, or misconduct penalties will be assessed in addition to the penalty shot.

Scoring

It is the responsibility of the referee—whose decision is final—to award all goals and assists. A goal is scored when the puck/ball has *completely* crossed the goal line. When a goal is scored, an *assist* is awarded to the player who passes the puck/ball to the player who scores the goal. No more than two assists are awarded per goal scored. Each goal and assist counts as one point on a player's scoring record. The referee will usually tell the official scorekeeper who scored the goal and assists, and the scorekeeper will write it down on the score sheet.

If an attacking player kicks the puck/ball directly into the net, or if the kicked puck/ball deflects off another player and/or the goalkeeper or is deliberately directed into the goal with any portion of the body other than the player's stick, the goal is disallowed. If a puck/ball deflects off an official and goes into the net, the goal also is disallowed. A goal can be scored only when the puck/ball is contacted by the player's stick below the waist.

After the game, the officials and both coaches will sign the official score sheet, and each will receive a copy. If there is any dispute over the score sheet, a coach must submit the dispute in writing to the league office.

The Team

An ice hockey or five-on-five roller hockey team roster may contain a maximum of 18 players (within the specific age grouping), plus no more than two goalkeepers. A four-on-four roller hockey team roster may contain a maximum of 12 players, including goalkeepers. These roster rules are meant to be the norm but are not written in stone. No player may appear on the rosters of two teams in the same league. In some leagues, younger players may play in a higher age division with written consent of their parents or guardians.

A team must choose one *captain* and two alternates, and the captain will be designated by a *C* on his or her jersey. The alternates will be designated by an *A* on their jerseys. A goalkeeper may not be designated the captain of the team. The captain is the sole voice of the team and will speak with the referee whenever the need arises. If the captain is penalized or suspended, one of the two remaining alternates will assume the captain's duties.

Whenever possible, all teams should be dressed in the same color and style jersey, socks, and pants. Each jersey should be numbered so that there is only one of each number per team. A starting lineup must be placed on the score sheet prior to the game starting. Any players who are not on the score sheet will not be allowed to participate in the game, no matter when they arrive.

Hockey Terms to Know

attempt to injure (deliberate injury)—An infraction resulting from a player or team official attempting to hit an opposing player, team official, or game official with the intent to cause injury.

back-checking—Attempts by forwards after losing possession of the puck/ball to slow or stop opponents' offensive attack.

boarding—An infraction resulting from a player checking an opponent violently into the boards. At the discretion of the referee, players shall be penalized, based upon the degree of violence of the impact with the boards, if they body check, cross-check, elbow, charge, or trip an opponent in a manner that causes the opponent to be thrown violently into the boards.

body checking—Intentional use of the body or part of the body to hinder an opponent. Body checking is prohibited in ice hockey for boys 10 years and younger, all girls and women classifications, and in roller hockey.

breakaway—A scoring opportunity that exists when players with full control of the puck/ball have no opposing players between themselves and the opposing goal.

broken stick—A stick that the referee deems unfit for play.

butt-ending—An infraction resulting from a player using the shaft of the stick above the upper hand to jab or attempt to jab an opposing player.

captain—A player, other than a goalkeeper, selected to represent the team with the officials.

charging—Taking more than two steps or strides to make contact with an opposing player.

creases—An enclosed space designated for the goalkeeper's protection and the referee's use. The lines which designate this space are considered part of the crease.

cross-checking—An infraction resulting from a player, holding the stick with both hands, checking an opponent by using the shaft of the stick with no part of the stick on the surface.

deke—A fake accomplished by moving the puck/ball or part of the body to one side, then moving in the opposite direction.

delayed offsides—A situation arising when an attacking player has preceded the puck/ball across the attacking blue line, but the defending team has gained possession of the puck/ball and is in position to bring it out of the defending zone without delay or contact with an attacking player.

dribbling—Another term for handling the puck/ball.

elbowing—An infraction resulting from a player using the elbow in any way to foul the opponent.

face-off—The action of the referee dropping the puck/ball between the sticks of two opposing players to start or resume play. A face-off begins when the referee indicates location of the face-off and ends when the puck/ball has been legally dropped.

forwards—A collective term for the center and wingers, who have the primary offensive objective of scoring a goal.

game disqualification—The result of a serious infraction in which a player is ejected from a game. This player must leave the area of the player's bench and may in no way direct, coach, or assist the team in any manner for the remainder of the game.

game suspension—The result of a serious infraction in which a player, coach, or manager is ineligible to participate in the next scheduled game.

HECC—An acronym for the Hockey Equipment Certification Council, an independent organization responsible for the development, evaluation, and testing of performance standards for protective ice hockey equipment.

heel of the stick—The point at which the shaft of the stick and the bottom of the blade meet.

high-sticking—An infraction resulting from a player carrying any part of the stick above the normal height of the waist.

holding—An infraction resulting from a player impeding the progress of an opponent.

hooking—An infraction resulting from a player using the stick blade in a *pulling or tugging* motion to impede the progress of an opponent.

icing—A stoppage of play that occurs when a team sends the puck down the length of the ice from its side of the red line.

kicking—An infraction resulting from a player deliberately using the skate(s) with a kicking motion to contact an opponent, with no intent to play the puck/ball.

kneeing—An infraction resulting from a player using the knee in any way to foul the opponent.

minor official—Officials appointed to assist the on-surface officials in conducting the game, including scorer, game timekeeper, penalty timekeeper, and goal judges.

offsides—An infraction resulting from players of an attacking team preceding the puck/ball into the attacking zone.

on-surface officials—Referees.

penalty—The result of an infraction of the playing rules by a player or team official.

penalty-killing unit—A group of players brought in to defend against a power play.

players—Members of the team physically participating in a game. The goalkeeper is considered a player unless rules specify otherwise.

poke checking—A sudden move goalkeepers make with the stick to contact the puck/ball with the stick blade.

possession—The state of a player other than a goalkeeper who has most recently come in contact with the puck/ball.

power play—A situation in which one team gains a numerical player advantage, usually following a penalty.

power-play goal—A goal scored while the opponent is skating a player down for a minor penalty.

protective equipment—Equipment worn by a player for the sole purpose of protecting against injury.

shorthanded—A condition in which a team is below the numerical strength of its opponent on the surface.

slashing—An infraction resulting from a player hitting an opponent with the stick while holding the stick with one or both hands. A player who swings the stick at an opponent without making contact is still guilty of slashing.

spearing—An infraction resulting from a player poking or attempting to poke an opponent with the toe of the stick blade while holding the stick with one or both hands.

stick checking—A technique involving players' use of the stick or blade to poke or strike an opponent's stick blade or a puck/ball in an opponent's possession.

team officials—Managers and support personnel, such as team manager, coach, assistant coach, trainer, equipment manager, and statistician.

Summary Test

Now that you have become familiar with the sports of ice and roller hockey, you should be able to answer a few basic questions:

1. The line that divides the surface into two equal parts in both ice and roller hockey is called the
   a. goal line
   b. red line
   c. blue line
   d. yellow line

2. What is scored when the puck/ball *completely* crosses the goal line is called a(n)
   a. point
   b. assist
   c. goal
   d. penalty

3. The surface on which both roller and ice hockey are played is called the
   a. goal
   b. boards
   c. face-off
   d. rink

4. List one major (a) and one minor (b) penalty common to both ice and roller hockey.
   a.
   b.

5. The number of minutes a minor penalty is assessed in ice or roller hockey for stop time is
   a. 3
   b. 2
   c. 5
   d. 10

6. The sole voice of the team who speaks with the referee whenever the need arises is the

   a. coach
   b. alternate captain
   c. goalkeeper
   d. captain

7. The standard number of players on the ice in ice hockey is

   a. five players plus a goalkeeper
   b. four players plus a goalkeeper
   c. five players only

8. A team's goal area in roller hockey is called the

   a. offensive zone
   b. defensive zone
   c. neutral zone
   d. trap zone

9. The player who is not allowed to be the captain is the

   a. right winger
   b. left winger
   c. center
   d. goalkeeper

10. The face-off that begins a game of either ice or roller hockey is called the

    a. center face-off
    b. defensive face-off
    c. offensive face-off

Answers: 1. b, 2. c, 3. d, 4. See Table 6.3, 5. b, 6. d, 7. a, 8. b, 9. d, 10. a

What Hockey Skills and Drills Should I Teach?

In unit 4 you learned how to teach skills and plan practices. This unit will help you apply that knowledge to teaching skating, stick handling, passing, shooting, offensive and defensive skills, and goalkeeping.

The following symbols will be used in figures throughout the remainder of the book to represent players, their movements, and the skills they are performing:

KEY

Coach   C$_o$

Center   C

Defense   D

Winger   W

Player   X or O

Player with puck/ball   X$_•$ or O$_•$

Pucks/balls   ▪▪▪

Pylon   △

Pass of puck/ball   ‑ഛഛഛഛഛ

Skating with puck/ball   ⋁⋁⋁⋀‑

Skating without puck/ball   ⟶

Skating backward   ::::::::::::::

Skating forward with stop   ———⊣

Skating backward with stop   ::::::::::::⊣

Shot   ⇒

Pivot   —º—

Pivot forward to backward   —º—::::::::

Pivot backward to forward   ::::::::—º⟶

Forward Skating

Hockey games demand too much concentration for players to be thinking about how to skate; therefore, skating is the most important skill to practice. Regular practice is the key to improving skating ability.

Three Phases of Skating

Skating involves three phases: drive, glide, and recovery.

Drive

In the drive phase, players generate power through a skating thrust to the side. The back leg extends fully, followed by a final push off the toe of the skate (see Figure 7.1a).

Glide

In the glide phase, athletes maintain the body over the glide foot to maximize each stride length. Shoulders line up over the knee, which lines up over the toes (see Figure 7.1b).

Recovery

In the recovery stage, players quickly bring the extended foot back under the body midline, which ensures that the hips are over the skates with each extension (see Figure 7.1c).

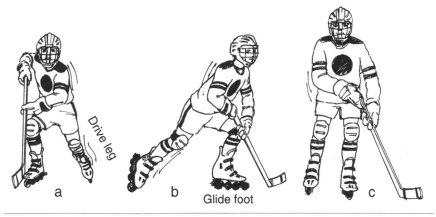

■ **Figure 7.1** Three phases of skating: (a) drive, (b) glide, and (c) recovery.

Generation of power is called the Z: All three joints are flexed, with knees over toes, chest over knees, and head up (see Figure 7.2).

■ **Figure 7.2** Generation of power: the Z.

Ready Position

The ready position is the building block for all skating. Just as a strong base gives a pyramid strength, the ready position provides a sturdy base for hockey players.

Players take the ready position with skates parallel and their feet shoulder-width apart, toes pointed straight ahead. Players bend the knees until they are in line with the skates' toes, lean the body slightly forward with the head up, and place one or two hands on the stick. The stick blade touches the rink surface.

Forward Striding

Players develop power with fast, short strides, then use longer and less frequent strides as speed increases. The stride starts with feet shoulder-width apart and all weight on the push foot. Players turn the push foot 35 to 40 degrees and push to the side and down, pressing the skate wheels or blade firmly against the rink surface. As they force the push foot out to the side, players push the knee of the other leg forward, extending the push skate leg as far as possible, through the ankle to the tip of the toe. After finishing the stride, players transfer weight to the forward foot (glide leg) and lift the push foot slightly over the rink surface. Players bend the knee of the back leg and pull it forward, close to the gliding foot, keeping it close to the rink surface and placing it back in its starting position to complete the recovery phase. Players then start the next stride with the opposite foot.

Striding Drills

Name. Stride Recovery Practice

Purpose. To practice forward striding maneuvers

Organization. Players assemble on one side of the rink, then skate across the rink surface, touching the knees to the surface with each stride.

Coaching Point. Make sure players point the glide foot straight ahead.

Variation. Players handle pucks/balls with their sticks.

Name. Skating Against Resistance

Purpose. To practice forward striding maneuvers

Organization. One player strides across the rink surface against a partner's resistance as they hold onto each others' sticks.

Coaching Point. Make sure the upper body, especially the head, remains in the proper position.

Variation. Vary resistance.

Name. Sculling

Purpose. To practice forward striding maneuvers

Organization. Players keep the glide foot on the rink surface and continually repeat the drive phase with the push foot, omitting the recovery phase.

Coaching Points. Focus on full drive leg extension and ensure that the glide foot remains straight.

Variation. Vary left and right foot.

Error Detection and Correction for Striding	
ERROR	**CORRECTION**
1. Head and shoulders not moving	1. Shift weight toward the stride foot.
2. Chest closed and no arch in the small of the back	2. Lift the head (look straight ahead) and maintain a comfortable arch in the small of the back.
3. No flexion at the back of the striding knee	3. Keep a 90-degree flexion at the back of the striding knee so that the thrust leg aligns the knee over the toe of that skate.
4. No rhythmic and complementary arm action	4. Use a rhythmic and complementary (front to back) arm action just like a natural walking arm swing.
5. No power generation in thrust	5. Generate power through a skating thrust to the side and a full extension of the push leg.

Starting Forward Striding

Teach your players two basic starts to begin a forward stride quickly and easily.

V-Start.   Players start in ready position, then turn the heels in and toes out, making a *V* with the skates as they lean slightly forward, putting weight on the front part of the foot. Players start to drive with either the right or left skate and alternate legs with each stride. Players make the first stride with each foot a short, driving stride, as if running. They make the next two strides slightly longer and reduce the angle between the rink surface and the wheels or blades. Players' third or fourth stride should have a wheel or blade angle of 35 to 40 degrees (see Figure 7.3a–b), and they should keep their skates near the rink surface for a quick recovery phase. Players gradually straighten up as speed increases.

■ **Figure 7.3** (a) V-start initial position and (b) third or fourth stride.

Crossover Start. Players start in ready position, then turn the head and place the stick in the direction of intended travel. Players then take the outside foot and step over the inside foot, staying low and not hopping. When the outside foot contacts the rink surface, players must keep it on the inside edge, using it as the driving foot in the push phase. Players take the original inside skate and place it on the rink surface near the driving skate, forming a *T* with the skates. Finally, players drive with the inside edge and continue the stride.

Starting Drills

Name. Starting Against Full Resistance

Purpose. To practice starting maneuvers

Organization. Using a V-start, one player strides across the rink surface against resistance of a partner as they hold each others' sticks.

Coaching Point. Make sure the upper body, especially the head, remains in proper position.

Variation. Vary resistance.

Name. Duck Walk/Toe Walk

Purpose. To practice starting maneuvers

Organization. Players control the inside edges while walking across the rink surface with skates open (heels together, toes pointing out) with blades/wheels flat on the surface. Then, while controlling the inside edges, they walk across the surface on the toes of their skates.

Coaching Point. Make sure players' skates approach the 90-degree mark.

Variation. Progress to running across the rink surface.

Name. Stepping Over the Sticks

Purpose. To practice starting maneuvers

Organization. Place three sticks in front of each group of players. Players must practice proper starting technique as they step over the sticks with short, quick steps before lengthening their strides (see Figure 7.4).

Coaching Points. Make sure players' skates approach the 90-degree mark and that players step onto the inside edge during the first step. Players' skate angle will decrease as steps increase. The hardest portion of this drill is the initial step—watch it carefully.

Variation. Progress to running across the rink surface.

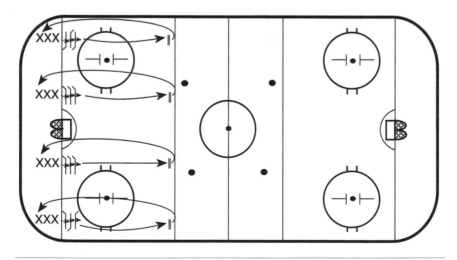

■ **Figure 7.4** Stepping Over the Sticks Drill.

Error Detection and Correction for Starting	
ERROR	CORRECTION
1. Improper upper body angle	1. Keep the upper body at a 60-degree angle to the rink surface. Keep the head and chest up and pointed down the rink.
2. Improper starting strides in attack phase	2. Make the first two starting strides in attack phase short with external rotation of the skate as close to 90-degrees as possible.
3. Improper edging	3. Push off inside edges and maintain shoulder-width skate bases.

Stopping Forward Striding

To become an effective hockey team, your players need to learn three basic stopping techniques. One of the most important elements of stopping is the preparation phase, which will be lengthy while players learn the various stops, but will shorten as they become more proficient with their techniques.

One Foot Drag.   This stop is primarily used in roller hockey. It will not stop players quickly and is better used as a slowing maneuver. To begin, players stop skating and glide into the approach. They need to assume the ready position and determine which foot will be the glide skate and which will do the stopping. Players should then allow the stopping skate to drag behind—not beside—the glide leg. They should drag the stopping skate on the inside edge of the wheels, placing direct pressure on it.

Quick Turn.   To execute the quick turn, players need to stop skating and glide into the approach in the ready position. Next, they should place the skate on the side they wish to turn toward directly in front of the other skate in a heel–toe arrangement (if turning right, the right foot must be in front). Players lead the stop by turning the head and shoulders in the direction they want to turn and bringing the arms and stick to the same side. Weight should be distributed as evenly as possible on both skates.

Players exert pressure on the outside edge of the leading skate and inside edge of the trailing skate. They should avoid sitting back on the skates, keeping them apart at shoulder-width around the quarter of a semicircle. Once the turn begins, players must press down with extreme force, causing the skates to produce a *quick turn*. As players stop, they will feel a force trying to propel them out of the stop, and they should be prepared to counter this force with proper body lean.

Two-Foot or Hockey Stop. This stopping maneuver is an advanced move, and players should initially turn just to the strong side. While staying in the basic stance, players glide on both skates as they approach the stopping point in ready position. Players must then turn the body at a right angle to the direction of travel (see Figure 7.5a). Players begin the stop by turning the shoulders (see Figure 7.5b), then the hips, as they swing the outside leg into braking position (see Figure 7.5c). The inside leg acts as a pivot, skates

a   b   c

Figure 7.5 Two-foot or hockey stop: (a) Turn the body at a right angle to the direction of travel; (b) begin the stop by turning the shoulders; then (c) turn the hips and swing the outside leg into braking position.

remain shoulder-width apart, and the inside skate travels slightly ahead of the outside skate in a heel–toe relationship. Weight is equally distributed on both skates. Next, players extend the legs vigorously while exerting pressure on the front part of the skates, using the inside edge of the outside skate and the outside edge of the inside skate. Pressure on the inside edge of the lead skate (outside skate) is especially important. Head and shoulders should remain straight, and players should avoid looking down at the rink surface. They should keep both hands on the stick, but avoid leaning on it.

Error Detection and Correction for Stopping

ERROR	CORRECTION
1. Improper foot placement	1. Keep feet shoulder-width apart with heel–toe alignment of skates.
2. Improper body alignment and weight transferal	2. Take a sitting down position with a good backward lean. Distribute weight evenly over both skates with pressure on the front of the skates.

Stopping Drills

Name. Reaction Stopping

Purpose. To practice stopping maneuvers

Organization. Players line up and skate down the rink surface. On the whistle, players react to the direction of the coach's stick and perform a specific stop to that side. The coach should be at least 15 feet in front of the players and point the stick to either side of the rink.

Coaching Points. Watch the initial preparation phase. Make sure players neither stand up during the preparation phase nor look down during the stop.

Variations. Start with a specific stop and work through all types. Practice stops in both directions.

Name.   Stopping Against Resistance

Purpose.   To practice stopping maneuvers

Organization.   Players pair off, and a lead player pulls a partner down the rink surface by holding onto the stick. The trailing player leans back and digs in the skate edges to stop the partner.

Coaching Point.   Watch for proper skate alignment.

Variation.   Start with very little resistance (the trailing player's body weight), then increase resistance as players become confident and more skilled.

Name.   Freeze Tag (for starting, skating, and stopping)

Purpose.   To practice stopping maneuvers

Organization.   Players skate against coaches, or specific lines of players skate against each other. One group attempts to tag all members of the other group. When tagged, players must freeze by stopping immediately and spreading their legs as widely as possible. Players become unfrozen only when a teammate slides head first, front to back through the widespread legs. Time to determine a winner.

Coaching Point.   Have some fun.

Variation.   Vary the direction and boundaries of skating (e.g., skating backward, skating forward inside the blue line only, skating backward in the neutral zone, etc.).

Turning

Hockey requires players frequently to make a transition from one direction to another. Although stopping techniques are effective for changing directions, players also need to learn three methods for turning on their skates.

Glide Turn

Similar to stopping, players begin a glide turn with a preparation phase. First, they stop skating and glide into an approach in ready position. Players place the skate on the side toward which they wish to turn directly in front of the other in a heel–toe relationship (see Figure 7.6a). Next, players turn the head and shoulders in the direction they wish to turn and bring the arms and stick to the same side (see Figure 7.6b). Players lean from the hips down, inside the half circle that their skates will make on the rink surface. Players should distribute weight evenly over both skates, keeping pressure on the outside edge of the leading foot and inside edge of the trailing foot (see Figure 7.6c).

a   b   c   (Outside edge) (Inside edge)

■ **Figure 7.6**   Glide turn: (a) Place the skate closest to the direction of the turn directly in front of the other skate in a heel–toe relationship; (b) turn the head and shoulders in the direction of the turn and bring the arms and stick to the same side; and (c) distribute weight evenly over both skates, keeping pressure on the outside edge of the leading foot and inside edge of the trailing foot.

Players should keep skates shoulder-width apart and center of gravity ahead of the skates to allow them to crossover after the tight turn and accelerate rapidly. Do not allow players to sit back on their skates. Once the skates have traveled a complete half circle on the rink surface, players execute a crossover start by bringing the back leg over the front leg to power out of the turn.

Error Detection and Correction for Glide Turns	
ERROR	CORRECTION
1. Improper foot placement and alignment	1. Place the inside skate ahead leading the turn.
2. Improper weight transfer and body lean	2. Use a strong sitting down action, lowering the body weight through the hips.
3. Improper upper body positioning	3. Turn head and shoulders first to assist body rotation through the turn.

Stride Turn

Players stop skating and glide into the approach in ready position. Players transfer weight over the support leg and lean into the direction of the stride, striding on the inside skate and pumping with outside skate as if sculling (see striding drills on page 95). The outside edge of the glide leg and inside edge of the thrust leg propel players through the turn, and they finish with low recovery skate placement and a strong toe-kick action.

Crossover Turn

Players use the crossover turn to maintain or increase speed while turning. First, players push the outside skate to the side, maintaining contact with the rink surface until the leg is fully extended. At the end of the push, players push down on the ball of the foot, using the ankles to get a little extra push from each stroke. Players lean into the turn from the waist down, pushing the hips into the turn and keeping the inside shoulder up. After the extension, players swing the outside leg over the inside skate. The outside skate should be parallel to the inside skate and slightly ahead of it. Players then push the inside skate to full extension outward under the body, using the outside edge. Once the skate is fully extended, it is returned quickly to its original position under the body, beside the outside skate. Players repeat this sequence throughout the turn, using equal force with each stroke. Players should practice this maneuver in both directions.

Error Detection and Correction for Crossover Turn

ERROR	CORRECTION
1. Problem staying in turn	1. Start with a glide turn using a strong sitting down action. Keep the stick to the inside of the turn and use the head and shoulders to assist body rotation.
2. Lack of power	2. Bend the knee of the glide foot and fully extend the push foot.

Turning Drills

Name. Open the Door

Purpose.   To practice turning maneuvers

Organization.   Ask players to put the right or left arm out in front of them. At a pylon they execute a glide turn while throwing the arm back and around, as if pushing open a door.

Coaching Point.   Emphasize shoulder and head turn.

Name. Free Leg Swing Over

Purpose.   To practice turning maneuvers

Organization.   Players begin by swinging the free leg back and forth across the support leg. Progress to kicking toward an outstretched stick and stepping over it.

Coaching Point.   Concentrate on proper skate alignment.

Variation.   Proceed to continuous strideovers.

Name. Game Turning Practice

Purpose.   To practice turning maneuvers

Organization.   Place a pylon about 20 feet above the lowest face-off dot. Players line up in the corners, then skate to the pylon and accelerate toward the middle of the rink (see Figure 7.7). Next, players skate quickly down to the face-off dot and make a turn from the outside in, toward the net. Players then skate across the mouth of the net with the stick down in position. Players switch lines, and each side comes together, forcing the players coming across the net to keep the head up.

Coaching Points. Concentrate on proper body positioning and alignment.

Variations. Use pucks/balls and a goalkeeper in the net. Also use as a relay race.

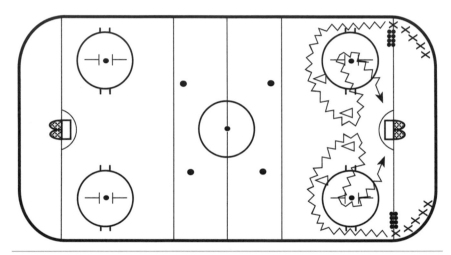

■ **Figure 7.7** Game Turning Practice Drill.

Pivoting

The pivot is a vital skating skill for helping your players make transitions. These transitions are especially important during games, when all players must be ready to play any position. For example, a center may be caught in a defense person's position. Players who pivot effectively will be better prepared for these situations.

To make a forward to backward pivot, players gain forward momentum and coast on the left skate. Players straighten up and rotate the right skate outward (as close to 180 degrees as possible) in a near heel down position. They start the turn by rotating the right shoulder backward, and the torso and hips follow. Players transfer weight from the left skate to the right skate, step down on the right skate, then take weight off the skates by going from bent knees to straight legs. Players finish the pivot by turning the left skate parallel with the right skate, then pushing to the side with the right skate and starting to skate backward. Teach your players to pivot to both sides.

Backward Skating

Most beginning ice and roller hockey players have problems skating backward, largely because they lean forward and bend the knees improperly. Most players need extra practice time to perfect the following backward maneuvers.

Backward Striding

Players begin in the ready position with feet close together and all weight on one foot. Using the front two wheels or the front portion of the blade, players push straight out to the side until the push leg is straight (see Figure 7.8 for a front and back view). When the stride is completed, players step to the opposite foot and lift the foot they have pushed with. Next, they bend the knee of the free leg and, keeping it close to the rink surface, pull it toward the skating leg. As the free foot nears the skating foot, players start striding with the opposite leg. They continue this alternating action with both feet, keeping weight over the striding leg.

■ **Figure 7.8** Backward striding: back and front views.

Push and Glide Backward

Players are moving backward with skates shoulder-width apart and all weight on one skate. Using the two front wheels or the front portion of the blade, players push straight out to the side until the push leg is fully extended (see Figure 7.9a). Players glide while the push leg recovers to a position under the body, close to the rink surface (see Figure 7.9b). The stride resembles a toe-in thrust, driven by the inside edge to form a C, which is called the C-cut of backward skating (see Figure 7.9c). Players continue the alternating action with both feet, keeping weight over the striding leg.

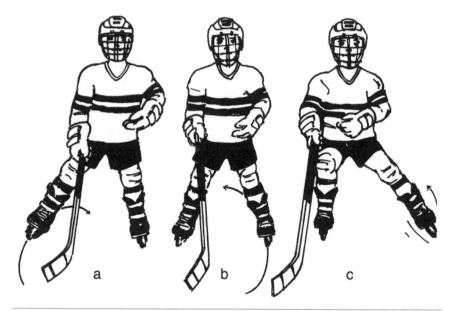

■ **Figure 7.9** Push and glide backward: (a) Push straight out to the side until the push leg is fully extended; (b) glide while the push leg recovers to a position under the body; and (c) drive stride by the inside edge to form a C.

Pivot (backward to forward)

Players begin moving backward. To turn to the left, players first transfer weight to the right skate, then rotate the left shoulder backward. The torso and hips follow. Players lift the left skate off the rink surface, turn it as close to 180 degrees as possible, and glide straight back on the right skate. Players then transfer weight to the left skate to complete the turn. At the moment of weight transfer, players must dig in the right skate and push hard, fully extending the right leg. Players are then ready to start forward striding. Teach players to accelerate out of the turn and to pivot to both sides.

Backward Crossover Stride

Players begin by moving backward with skates shoulder-width apart and weight evenly distributed over both skates. Next, they C-cut with the lead foot and from a ready gliding position, lift the outside skate and step over the inside foot. Then players push off of the outside edge of the skate (power generation), and transfer the weight from the outside edge of the push foot to the inside edge of the support leg and complete the maneuver. The stepping action continues until the players are in the desired direction.

Backward One-Foot Stop and T-Push

Players begin moving backward, then extend the left leg and transfer weight to the right leg. The left leg begins to swing back, and the shoulders, hips, and legs turn in a counterclockwise direction as players plant the left skate in a braking position, using the inside edge of the skate (see Figure 7.10a). Players bend the left knee and transfer weight from the right leg to the left leg. The majority of resistance comes from the left skate. The right skate and knee move under the body, placing the skates in position for a T-push start (see Figure 7.10b).

V-Stop for Backward Skating

Players spread the feet shoulder-width apart with the toes of both skates turned out and heels turned in (see Figure 7.11). They lean forward, forcing the inside edges of the skates against the rink surface. Players should keep a slight bend in the knees during the first phase of the stop, then extend the legs during the final phase, exerting pressure through the skates' wheels or blades. After stopping, players should be in ready position, prepared to skate in any direction.

■ **Figure 7.10** Backward one-foot stop and T-push: (a) Swing the left leg back, turning the shoulders, hips, and legs in a counterclockwise direction, and plant the left skate in a braking position using the inside edge of the skate; and (b) bend the left knee, transferring weight from the right to the left leg, and move the right skate and knee under the body, placing the skates in position for a T-push start.

■ **Figure 7.11** V-stop for backward skating.

Error Detection and Correction for Backward Skating

ERROR	CORRECTION
1. Improper body position	1. Hold the trunk more upright than in forward skating and flex at the hip, knee, and ankle. Maintain a good sitting down position.
2. Improper weight transfer	2. Posture should allow for total body mass to be located over the ball of the foot and well within the base for support.
3. Improper skating stride	3. Direct force with a ball-to-heel thrust, forming a C-cut with the striding skate.

Backward Skating Drills

Name. Loading and Unloading the Thrust Leg

Purpose. To practice backward skating maneuvers

Organization. Players begin backward slalom skating, then progress to alternate skates dropping from the thrust leg while transferring weight to the glide leg. Players demonstrate leaping and knee-collapse action from left leg to right leg by hopping from skate to skate while moving backward.

Coaching Point. Make sure players demonstrate the loading and unloading of the knee.

Name. Backward Stopping and Starting

Purpose. To practice backward skating maneuvers

Organization. Players skate backward across either the length or width of the rink surface and on the whistle perform a stop. After stopping, players assume a backward starting position, and on the word "Go" they perform a backward start.

Coaching Points. Emphasize the V-position of skates as body weight shifts toward the ball of the foot. T-position can be used if predominant right or left direction starting will follow. The center of the body mass must stay over the midfoot when stopping and starting.

Variation. Progress to a mirror (shadow) drill. In this drill, one player is the leader and the other players follow his/her moves.

Name. Partner Tug-of-War

Purpose. To practice backward skating maneuvers

Organization. Players find partners and face each other. Each player should be holding a butt-end or stick shaft in each hand, the end of which the partner then grabs. On the whistle or the word "Go," each player tries to pull the partner closer while skating away backward.

Coaching Points. Make sure players use proper backward skating and starting techniques.

Variation. Use the face-off circles: The first player to drag a partner out of the circle wins.

Basic Skills

The skill work covered in this section applies to both ice and roller hockey. The primary difference is that a roller hockey puck is usually lighter than an ice hockey puck. These basic skills should be practiced frequently by all players, allowing them enough time to perfect their skills.

Grip

The grip used to hold the stick is very important to players' success. To grip properly, the top hand must be at the end of the stick, just before the butt end. The lower hand should be 20 to 30 centimeters down the shaft—about shoulder length from the upper hand. To ensure that your players use the proper distance, take the elbow of the bottom hand and place it on top of the thumb of the top hand, which is holding onto the butt end of the stick. Have players rest the forearm of the bottom hand on the stick shaft, then grab the shaft with the fingers of the bottom hand. This should be the proper distance between hands. The *V* formed by the thumb and forefinger should point straight up the shaft (see Figure 7.12). Players must keep the head up and use peripheral vision to look at the puck/ball. Allow younger players to look and feel for the puck/ball in the beginning.

■ **Figure 7.12**   Grip used to hold the stick.

Stationary Puck/Ball Handling

Puck/ball handling, or *dribbling*, while the player is stationary may not seem to fit a hockey game scenario, but players should practice this maneuver to allow total concentration on puck/ball handling without concerns about skating. First, players need to assume the ready position. Next, with both hands on the stick and the stick blade on the rink surface, players move the puck/ball from side to side by rolling the wrists and shifting weight to the same skate that the puck/ball is on. This action cups the stick blade on both the forehand and backhand sides, providing better control. To roll the wrists, players turn the forehand side of the blade downward and the backhand side upward, then reverse direction. Players handle (dribble) the puck/ball in the middle of the blade while keeping the arms relaxed and away from the upper body (see Figure 7.13). Puck/ball control must be smooth, rhythmic, and quiet. Watch for players' stick blades banging on the rink surface as a sign that they are not in control of their sticks (check hand placement if this occurs).

■ **Figure 7.13**   Stationary puck/ball handling.

Puck/Ball Handling With Movement

Follow the technique described previously for stationary puck/ball handling, but players must place the stick blade on a slight angle so that the puck/ball is propelled forward and to the side. Players will find comfortable angles that they wish to use.

Sweep Passes

There are two types of sweep passes: forehand and backhand. The sweep pass is a normal pass that gets its name from the sweeping motion of the stick (like sweeping the floor with a broom).

Forehand Sweep Pass

Players begin in the ready position, then bring the puck/ball beyond the plane of the body (slightly behind the back skate) with the puck/ball in the middle of the stick blade (see Figure 7.14a), which should be at a right angle to the target. Players keep body weight on the back leg, head up, and eyes on the target (see Figure 7.14b). Pulling with the top hand and pushing with the bottom hand, players propel the puck/ball toward the target by sweeping the arms (see Figure 7.14c). While propelling the puck/ball, players transfer weight from the rear leg to the front leg, almost using a stepping motion (see Figure 7.14d). Players' sticks follow through low and toward the target, and players immediately prepare to receive a return pass.

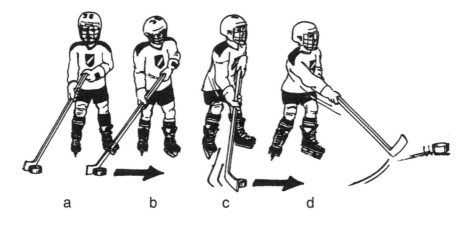

a   b   c   d

■ **Figure 7.14** Forehand sweep pass: (a) Bring the puck/ball beyond the plane of the body with the puck/ball in the middle of the stick blade; (b) keep the body weight on the back leg, head up, and eyes on the target; (c) propel the puck/ball toward the target by sweeping the arms; and (d) transfer the weight from the rear to the front leg.

Backhand Sweep Pass

Like the forehand sweep pass, players' hands remain well away from the body. Players bring the puck/ball beyond the plane of the body while shifting weight to the back leg (see Figure 7.15a), keeping the head up and eyes on the target. Players cup the backhand side of the stick blade over the puck/ball. Next, players shift weight from the back foot to the front and sweep the stick across the body to propel the puck/ball (see Figure 7.15b). The stick follows through low, and players immediately prepare to receive a return pass (see Figure 7.15c).

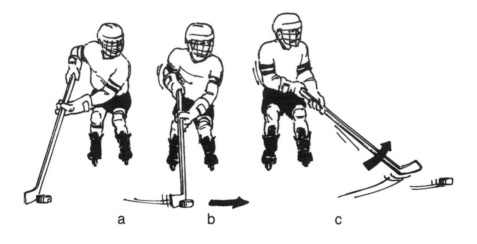

a   b   c

■ **Figure 7.15** Backhand sweep pass: (a) Bring the puck/ball beyond the plane of the body while shifting weight to the back leg, keeping the head up and eyes on the target; (b) shift the weight from the back foot to the front and sweep the stick across the body; and (c) follow through with the stick low and prepare to receive a return pass.

Flip Pass

The flip is a situational pass used to send the puck/ball over an obstacle (e.g., an opponent's stick, body, leg, etc.) to a target. To attempt a flip pass (or saucer pass as it is sometimes called), players start with the puck/ball on the stick heel (backhand or forehand) while they hold the stick just in front of the body. Next, players try to slide the puck/ball off the stick blade from the heel to the toe while following through with an upward motion. This action should cause a puck to spin and fly like a saucer in the air and cause a ball to spin like a top while flying over an obstacle toward the target.

Receiving Passes

Just as important as teaching proper techniques for sending passes is helping players learn proper methods for receiving them.

Receiving Passes on the Forehand

To receive passes on the forehand, players keep the head up and eyes on the puck/ball carrier. Pass receivers must present a target with the stick blade, which must be in contact with the rink surface. Once passers release the puck/ball, receivers' blades must remain at a 90-degree angle to the direction of the puck/ball. Players must watch the puck/ball throughout the pass reception (see Figure 7.16), and as the puck/ball makes contact with the stick blade, players should provide a cushioning effect with the blade. Once players control the puck/ball, they should be prepared to pass. If players provide the proper amount of cushioning, the stick blade should be in the ready position to give a pass immediately.

■ **Figure 7.16** Receiving passes on the forehand.

Receiving Passes on the Backhand

To receive a pass on the backhand, players keep the head up and eyes on the passer and the puck/ball. They should follow the previously stated techniques for forehand receiving, but should substitute the backhand portion of the stick blade for the forehand portion. Finally, players need to cup the blade of the stick over the puck/ball (see Figure 7.17).

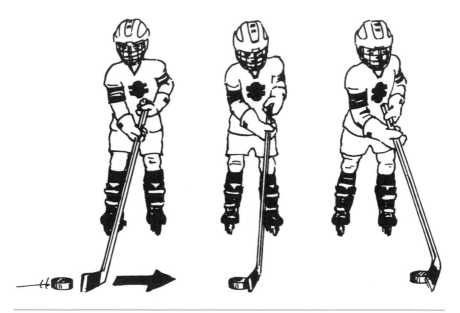

■ **Figure 7.17** Receiving passes on the backhand.

Passing Drills

Name. Star Passing on the Circles

Purpose. To practice stationary passing maneuvers

Organization. Five players line up on the line around the face-off circle. One player is given a puck/ball and told to pass to a player directly across the circle. Each player continues in the same manner, but players are not allowed to pass back to the player who just passed to them.

Coaching Point. Make sure players use proper stationary passing techniques.

Variation. Play Monkey in the Middle in the same formation. The only additional rule is that players cannot pass to someone next to them.

Name. Two-On-Zero Passing

Purpose. To practice movement passing maneuvers

Organization. Players pair up and start in one corner of the rink. Each pair receives a puck/ball. On command each pair tries to complete as many passes as possible while they skate two-on-zero down to the other end of the rink. You can also run this drill from opposite corners of the rink.

Coaching Point. Make sure players use proper movement passing techniques.

Variation. Place obstacles between the two players to force them to look up and react to what is ahead.

Name. Head Player Passing

Purpose. To practice movement passing maneuvers

Organization. Form four groups of players, each of which lines up on one of the offside face-off dots (see Figure 7.18). Each group faces the middle of the rink. One player starts to skate toward the group that is in the same zone on the opposite side of the rink. The first player in the stationary group makes a pass to the player skating toward the group. Once the pass is completed, the player with the puck/ball makes a quick turn up the rink surface going in on a one-on-zero. At the same time the player who made the pass starts to skate toward the group to which he or she just passed. The next person in that group passes to this player, who receives it then makes a quick turn up the rink surface and goes in on a one-on-zero. The drill continues as each passer becomes the next skating receiver. After taking the shot, the player goes to the end of the line on the opposite side of the rink from which he/she started in the same zone from which the shot was taken.

Coaching Points. Make sure players use proper skating and passing techniques.

Variations. Add goalkeepers and allow a shot or add defense players to have a one-on-one in the offensive zone.

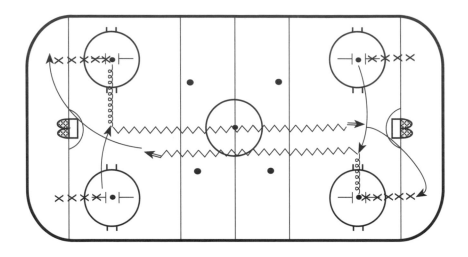

■ **Figure 7.18** Head Player Passing Drill.

Name. Four Corner Passing (Passing Around the Horn)

Purpose. To practice passing and receiving maneuvers

Organization. All but three players line up single file in one of the corners. Position the remaining three players in a box formation in the same zone (see Figure 7.19). The first player is 20 to 25 feet directly ahead of the player in the corner, and the second player is directly across the width of the rink from player one. Player three is in the same position but on the opposite side of the player starting the drill in the corner. The player starting the drill takes a puck/ball and passes it to player one; player one passes to player two; and player two passes to player three. While these players pass the puck/ball, the original player skates out around player one and down the middle of the zone, receiving a pass in motion from player three, then attempting a shot on goal.

Coaching Points. Make sure players use proper skating, passing, and receiving techniques.

Variation. Pass and follow rather than passing around the horn.

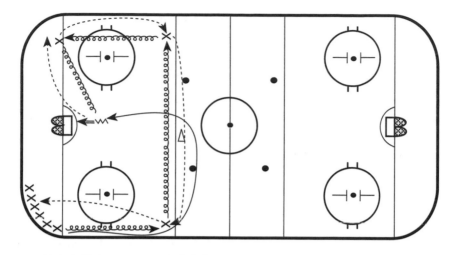

■ **Figure 7.19**   Four Corner Passing Drill.

Open Surface Carry

Players use this maneuver in open surface when they will not be challenged by opponents. Players need to control the stick with the top hand only and push the puck/ball slightly ahead with the bottom edge of the stick blade by straightening the arm at the elbow, making sure they keep the puck/ball in contact with the stick blade. It is important for the hand controlling the stick to be on top of the stick, away from the upper body. You can practice this maneuver on both forehand and backhand sides and use full rink surface carries or one-on-zero drills.

Shooting

Because scoring goals is the basic offensive objective of hockey, shooting is one of the most practiced maneuvers in the game. Players must understand these important concepts:

1. No matter which shot players take, proper form is extremely important.
2. Accuracy is the second most important factor in shooting.

3. Quickness is a kind of secret weapon (if everyone—especially the goalkeeper—has time to prepare, effectiveness is lost).
4. Shot variety makes a difference (if players take the same shot every time, they lose the element of surprise).

We have intentionally omitted the slap shot from this book because of its inaccuracy, the length of time required to take the shot, and the inability of most young players to produce the lower and upper body strength needed to master it.

Forehand Sweep (Wrist) Shot

Players should use the same basic grip as in passing, bringing the puck/ball beyond the plane of the body and keeping it in contact with the stick blade until they are ready to release it. Players then shift weight to the back foot. While sweeping the puck/ball forward, they transfer weight to the front foot (see Figure 7.20a). Players' heads must be up with eyes on the target (see Figure 7.20b). To release the puck/ball, players snap and roll the wrists, pulling the top hand and pushing the bottom hand. Next, they follow through low for a low shot and high for a high shot. Players keep the wrists cocked until the moment of release and then snap them through the shot.

Figure 7.20 Forehand sweep (wrist) shot: (a) Transfer weight forward and (b) keep the head up, with the eyes on the target.

Backhand Sweep Shot

The backhand sweep shot is the same as the wrist shot, only taken from the backhand position. It is extremely important that players keep the knee bent and get most of their power by transferring weight to the opposite foot.

Flip Shot

Think of a flip shot as a clearing shot or pass. It is mainly used to relieve pressure in the defensive end by throwing or flipping the puck/ball out of the zone. The primary focus should be on lofting the puck/ball over any opponents and out of the zone, not on speed or accuracy. To practice this maneuver, players should place the hands in the proper position on the stick shaft, open—not cup—the forehand portion of the stick blade, and attempt to lift the puck/ball using a quick, sharp upward movement of the open-faced blade.

Snap Shot

Think of this shot as a wrist shot with a little extra snap at the end. Players use the same techniques as the wrist shot, but just prior to releasing the puck/ball, they should forcefully *snap* through the puck/ball. Players need to strike the rink surface 1 to 2 inches behind the puck/ball. Hand position, follow through, upper body position and weight transfer remain the same as in the wrist shot.

Error Detection and Correction for Shooting

ERROR	CORRECTION
1. Improper weight transfer causing a weak or inaccurate shot	1. Place the weight on the back foot stepping through to the front foot while shooting.
2. Improper hand positioning	2. Hands should be shoulder-width apart.
3. Hands too close to upper body, causing improper wrist action	3. Hands need to have room to flow. Hands and arms need to be out comfortably away from the chest and waist.

Shooting Drills

Name. Shooting Practice

Purpose. To practice several shooting maneuvers

Organization. Players line up 10 to 20 feet from the boards at least one stick length away from each other, all around the rink perimeter. Keep players away from the corners. Provide players with at least one puck/ball each and instruct them to use only the shot you have chosen. Players choose a target on the board and practice taking shots at it.

Coaching Points. Make sure players use proper shooting techniques; view all of your players. Instruct players to always keep their eyes on the target.

Variations. Vary the height and distance of each target. Practice both low and high shots.

Name. Figure Eight Shooting

Purpose. To practice forehand and backhand shooting maneuvers while in motion

Organization. Divide players into four groups, positioning each in one of the four corners of the rink (see Figure 7.21). Make sure that each player has a puck/ball. On your command players advance one at a time around the face-off circle in front of them and take a shot on net. Players then skate to the adjacent circle, pick up a puck/ball, skate around that circle, and take a shot on net. This drill should give each player an opportunity to take a forehand and backhand shot.

Coaching Points. Make sure players use proper skating and shooting techniques and that goalkeepers have enough recovery time between players.

Variation. Once proficient skating forward, players should skate backward.

Name. Flip Ins

Purpose. To practice flip shot maneuvers

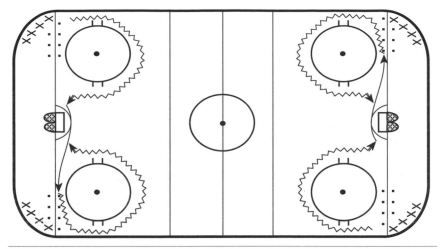

■ **Figure 7.21**   Figure Eight Shooting Drill.

Organization.   Players each take a puck/ball and line up just outside the offensive zone. One at a time they try to flip the puck/ball into the opposite side corner (see Figure 7.22).

Coaching Points.   Make sure players use proper techniques and that pucks/balls go high and deep enough.

Variation.   Practice from the defensive end.

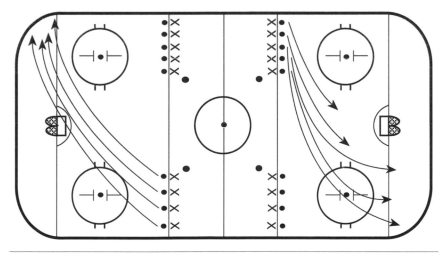

■ **Figure 7.22**   Flip Ins Drill.

Checking Techniques

Because of the lack of body checking in roller hockey and in the lower age levels of ice hockey, this discussion focuses on stick checking.

Stick Checking (including the poke check)

This maneuver requires players to use the stick blade to poke or strike an opponent's stick blade or a puck/ball in an opponent's possession. The stick check is generally executed with one hand— usually the top hand—on the stick shaft. To execute the stick check, players quickly extend the arm with the stick toward the puck/ball. Players must not lunge at the puck/ball, and they must remain in the proper skating position. The stick blade must remain on the rink surface to make contact with the puck/ball.

Lifting the Opponent's Stick

Players use this stick check when coming up from behind an opponent who is carrying the puck/ball. With an element of surprise, players slide the stick under the opponent's stick and lift quickly (see Figures 7.23a–b). Players must bring the stick back to the rink surface quickly to recover the puck/ball (see Figure 7.23c). Players should immediately skate away from the opposing player.

Covering the Opponent

Players execute this technique differently, depending on whether the opponent has the puck/ball. If the opponent does not have the puck/ball, players should keep themselves between the opponent and the puck/ball, staying within one stick length of the opponent to cover that player effectively. If the opposing player has the puck/ball, then players should try to force the opposition to the outside portions of the rink where the puck/ball carrier will eventually run out of skating room. Once players get within a comfortable distance, they should do one of the stick-checking maneuvers mentioned previously. Remind players not to lunge after the puck/ball.

■ **Figure 7.23** Lifting the opponent's stick: (a and b) Slide the stick under the opponent's stick and lift quickly; and (c) recover the puck/ball.

Checking Drills

Name. Corner Dump Ins

Purpose. To practice basic noncontact checking maneuvers

Organization. Players line up in two lines about a stick length apart, just outside the offensive zone (see Figure 7.24). Designate one player as offense and another as defense. On your command a puck/ball is dumped into the corner. The defensive player waits at the line briefly, allowing the offensive player to gain control of the puck/ball. Then the defensive player tries to stick check and cover the puck/ball carrier. The offensive player should try to maintain a predetermined path as long as possible. The drill continues for a set amount of time or distance.

Coaching Points.   Make sure players use proper stick and covering techniques and that the offensive player maintains a predetermined path at first.

Variation.   Progress to one-on-one in the corner with the offensive player trying to score.

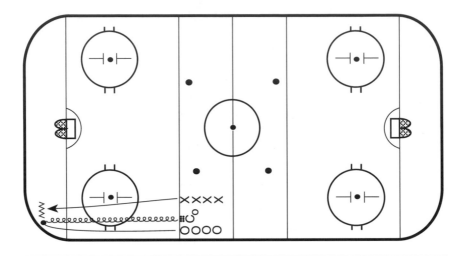

■ **Figure 7.24**   Corner Dump Ins Drill.

Name.   One-On-One in the Circle

Purpose.   To practice basic noncontact checking maneuvers

Organization.   Divide players into pairs. One pair stands inside the face-off circle, and one player has a puck/ball. On your command each pair plays a mini one-on-one keep-away game. The object is to have control of the puck/ball when the predetermined time for the drill ends.

Coaching Points.   Make sure players use proper skating and checking techniques and that they stay inside the circles.

Variations.   Use whole sections of the rink surface and establish teams with a predetermined number of pucks/balls. Also play a game with the same premise as musical chairs but with pucks/balls.

Goaltending

Goalkeeper is the position coaches most frequently neglect when developing players' skills. Coaches must spend time with goalies to help them attain and improve on the basic skills they need to succeed.

Differences Between Ice and Roller Hockey Goaltending

The biggest difference between ice and roller hockey goaltending is that ice hockey goalkeepers can actually slide their skates across the ice to move laterally. The blades are sharpened with a very small hollow specifically for this purpose. Roller hockey goalies must pick up their skates to move laterally, creating a second when they are vulnerable to be scored upon. To minimize this risk, goalkeepers need to master the T-push maneuver. Another big difference between the two sports is that ice hockey goalies can execute a two-pad slide with some ease. In roller hockey, depending on the surface, goalkeepers may need to apply more force to move the same distance.

Stance

Goalkeepers must start in the ready position; otherwise, the moves they must master become more difficult to perform. The ready position begins with weight on the middle of the skates to the heels, legs shoulder-width apart, knees bent, rear down, shoulders back, stick in front of and between the skates, gloves off the pads and in front of the body, and catch glove above the hip (see Figure 7.25).

Movement

You must teach lateral movement to goalkeepers so they can cover the entire net without leaving a large shooting space for the opposition. Break the movement down into short and long distances. The T-push is good for long distance lateral movements, and the shuffle step is good for short distance lateral movements.

■ **Figure 7.25** Goaltender stance.

Error Detection and Correction for Goalkeeper Ready Position	
ERROR	CORRECTION
1. Pads too far apart and goalies too much on the inside skate edges	1. Correct the V-position of skates and pads. Stay on middle edges of blades/wheels.
2. Elbow of catch glove too tight to body	2. Keep five hole (hole between pads) small. Move elbow away from body.
3. Gloves resting on pads creating overlapping coverage	3. Move gloves away from body (to the side).
4. Shoulder too far forward	4. Keep weight over the middle of the skates (balls of the feet).

Shuffle Step

To execute the shuffle step, goalkeepers remain in ready position while shuffling the feet with small steps either right or left. Goalies should keep the shoulders square and the back to the net.

T-Push

To use the T-push, goalkeepers turn the lead foot in the direction they wish to go and push off with the inside edge of the other foot. Once goalies reach the desired location or distance, they stop and assume the ready position.

Telescoping

Telescoping is goalkeepers' art of forward and backward movement. Goalies move forward by pushing off the inside edge of one foot, to obtain power, and then gliding in the ready position to the desired position or distance. To move backward, goalkeepers use the inside edge of one foot to draw the letter C on the rink surface and then glide in the ready position to the desired position or distance.

▦ Movement Drills ▦

Name. Side-To-Side Shooting

Purpose. To practice lateral movements

Organization. Position two shooters 10 to 15 feet in front of the net, 10 to 20 feet apart, and a goalkeeper in the middle of the net in ready position. On your whistle the two shooters pass the puck/ball back and forth, slowly at first, while the goalkeeper practices the T-push and shuffle step movements. After a predetermined number of passes the player with the puck/ball shoots it.

Coaching Points. Make sure goalkeepers stay in the ready position and use both lateral movement techniques. Also make sure that players move the puck/ball slowly at first to allow goalies to concentrate on proper movement rather than the actual shot.

Variation. Have players form a semicircle using three shooters. Allow the center player always to get the puck/ball back before passing to the other side, forcing goalkeepers to get back to the middle of the net in the ready position.

Name. Challenge and Retreat

Purpose. To allow goalkeepers to practice forward and backward telescoping movements

Organization. Place players in one corner of the rink with pucks/balls. Place another player 15 to 20 feet in front of the middle of the net. Have the goalkeeper start on the side of the player in the corner (see Figure 7.26). That player passes out to the player in front of the net, and the goalie practices challenging the pass receiver, who then shoots the puck/ball. After the shot the goalkeeper must retreat by skating backward to the net, restarting the drill. Run the drill from both sides of the rink.

Coaching Points. Monitor goalkeepers' quickness and challenge position. Do not allow goalkeepers to come out of the net too far. Also watch that goalkeepers do not cheat by leaving the net too soon. Begin with slow passes and concentrate on goaltending techniques.

Variations. Vary the number of shooters and direction of passes. Also vary the number of passes before the shot.

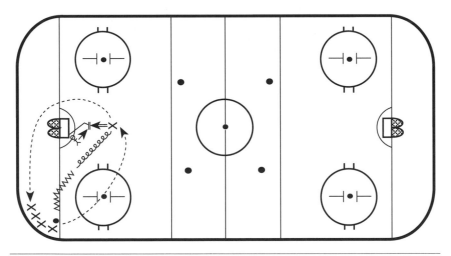

■ **Figure 7.26** Challenge and Retreat Drill.

Common Save Techniques

Now that the players can balance in the ready position and move around the crease, they need to know how to use the equipment they wear to stop the puck/ball.

Stick Saves

Using a firm grip, goalkeepers hold the stick in the blocker glove hand, just above the paddle (widened portion of the goal stick) on the shaft. The most important part of the stick save is that the blade of the stick must remain on the rink surface at all times to stop the low shot; the blade should not rest on the front of the skates (see Figure 7.27). A stick save made on low shots should angle shots away from the front of the net, toward the corners. The stick should cushion shots aimed right at goalkeepers. During high shots goalies use the stick like a baseball bat, directing the stick paddle to the puck/ball. Remind goalkeepers to direct the puck/ball away from the goal mouth.

■ **Figure 7.27** In preparation for a stick save, the blade must remain on the rink surface.

============= **Stick Save Drill** =============

Name. Stick Saves (low and high)

Purpose. To practice making stick saves and clearing pucks/balls away from the goal mouth

Organization. Place several shooters 10 to 20 feet from the net and ask them to shoot the puck/ball either high or low, depending on the stick save you want to practice. Allow a predetermined number of shots, and after the last shot review with the goalkeeper where the pucks/balls lie on the rink surface.

Coaching Points.   Make sure that goalies keep the stick blade on the surface and return to ready position between shots. Correct common problems and monitor the buffer zone between the stick and the skates.

Variation.   Stagger players across the rink and alternate shots side to side, forcing goalkeepers to travel the entire length of the net to set up prior to the shot.

Error Detection and Correction for Stick Saves	
ERROR	CORRECTION
1. Raising the stick blade off the rink surface	1. Force the stick down to the surface. Allow the hand to slide up and down the shaft of the stick.
2. Failure to keep a buffer between the stick blade and the skates	2. Keep at least 6 inches between the blade of the stick and the toes of the skates.
3. Failing to clear pucks/ balls away from the goal mouth	3. Angle the stick to the side slightly so the puck/ball is directed at the corners.

Poke Checks

A *poke check* is a sudden move goalkeepers make with the stick to contact the puck/ball with the stick blade. There are three basic types of poke checks: standing, power, and diving. Goalies make the standing poke check by thrusting the stick out toward the puck/ball, almost like throwing the stick at the puck/ball, without letting go of the shaft. The goal stick must have a large butt end or a wad of tape on the end of the shaft to stop the stick from sliding out of the hand. After thrusting the stick at the puck/ball, goalkeepers draw the stick back quickly and assume the ready position. The other two poke checks are similar in execution, but are started in different body positions. The power poke check is executed with the stick-side knee down. For a diving poke check goalies thrust the stick at the puck/ball, then follow with the body. Once the body starts to slide on the rink surface, goalkeepers must cover all the surface possible, so they spread the legs in a large *V*, pointing the toes toward the direction they are sliding.

Poke Check Drill

Name. Poke Check Practice

Purpose. To practice the different types of poke checks

Organization. Place players with pucks/balls in each corner, and from alternating directions have them skate in front of the net just above the crease (see Figure 7.28). While players skate across the net, goalkeepers practice the different types of poke checks.

Coaching Points. Monitor the stance prior to, during, and after the poke check. Look for quick, surprising movements and contact with the puck/ball.

Variations. Practice all types of poke checks.

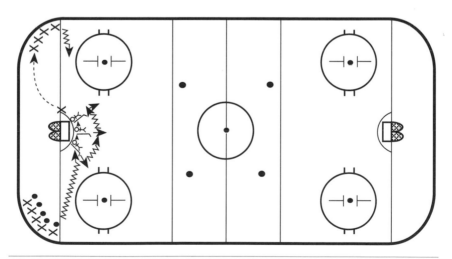

■ **Figure 7.28** Poke Check Practice Drill.

Skate Saves

This discussion of skate saves is broken down into two different types: standing and one-knee skate saves. If goalies can reach the puck/ball with a standing skate save, they can also reach it with the stick. Because they should attempt the stick save first, goalkeepers should use the standing skate save only as a backup to the stick save. To execute this save properly, goalkeepers should point the toe of the skate they wish to move toward the puck/ball and push off the inside edge of the opposite skate, causing the turned foot to roll or glide across the rink surface. The stick must be in front of the skate trying to make the save.

Goalkeepers execute the one-knee skate save while resting on the inside knee. They must place all weight on the inside knee, keep the skate wheels or blade on the rink surface, snap the leg out, keep the stick down and glove up, and try not to fall backward. Goalkeepers should avoid using the gloves to push themselves up.

Error Detection and Correction for Standing Skate Saves

ERROR	CORRECTION
1. Difficulty recovering	1. Roller hockey goalkeepers will have problems with this save if they leave the brakes on their skates. The brake or plastic brake holder will hinder goalkeepers from extending the legs for the skate save.
2. Inadequate range for the save	2. Know the limitations (range) of the save and where you are in the net.
3. Slow recovery past the initial save	3. Practice recovering from a save just as much as practicing the save. Practice making saves from multiple shooters to emphasize quick recovery.

Error Detection and Correction for One-Knee Skate Saves

ERROR	CORRECTION
1. First movement is up with the shoulders	1. Begin in the ready position, then drop down on the inside knee keeping the upper body still.
2. Leaning away from the shot (not covering the net with the upper body)	2. Keep the upper body straight and upright while keeping the shoulders square to the puck/ball.
3. Sitting back on the inside skate	3. Rest on the knee.
4. No snap to the extended leg	4. Quickly extend the leg making the save with a snap and recover quickly.

Skate Save Drills

Name. Puck/Ball Soccer

Purpose. To familiarize goalkeepers with contacting the puck/ball with their skates

Organization. Place two goalkeepers in a small area (e.g., the face-off circle) without sticks and have them play soccer against each other.

Coaching Point. Monitor how goalkeepers strike the puck/ball with the skates, and make sure they use the inside edges.

Variations. Use a larger area or incorporate more players.

Name. Controlled Skate Saves

Purpose. To familiarize goalkeepers with making skate saves

Organization. Place a goalkeeper in the net and have several players 10 to 20 feet away from the front of the net take low shots that remain on the rink surface.

Coaching Points. Watch how goalkeepers strike the puck/ball with the skates. Make sure that they use the inside edges and that the stick leads the save.

Variation.   Take the stick away only when you are sure that goalkeepers are proficient at leading the save with the stick.

Butterfly Pad Save

Goalies use this save when there is a large amount of traffic in front
of the net or against a deking forward. Advantages over the skate
save are that goalkeepers can cover more area, and they have better
chances of guessing correctly. One of the greatest disadvantages of
this save is that while using the pads goalies give up more rebounds
in front of the net.

The most important aspect of the butterfly is covering the upper
portion of the net with the goalkeeper's upper body. To perform
this save properly, goalies drop to the knees while pointing the toes
out, creating a *V*. The goal is to cover as much rink surface as possible with this *V* while keeping the upper body in the ready position
(see Figure 7.29).

■ **Figure 7.29**   Butterfly pad save.

There is also a half-butterfly variation of this save performed by
dropping one knee instead of both.

Error Detection and Correction for Butterfly Pad Saves	
ERROR	CORRECTION
1. Weight not on knees	1. Keep the weight on the knees with the upper body upright.
2. Improper pad placement	2. Keep pads flat on the surface by driving the knees down.
3. Improper stick placement	3. Cover the opening between the legs with the stick. The stick should not be angled, but straight up and down. As always keep the stick about 3 to 6 inches in front of the pads.

Goalkeeper Saving Drill

Name. Russian Reverse

Purpose. To familiarize goalkeepers with pad saves

Organization. Goalkeepers lie on the back with feet toward the goal line and the head toward the center of the rink surface. You kneel with pucks/balls 5 to 10 feet from goalkeepers, and they raise the legs into the air, arms outstretched to each side. While you throw pucks/balls toward the net, goalies try to hit them with the pads or gloves. The reaction goalkeepers must make is a reverse of the norm. (The Russian philosophy on this drill is that if an individual can do something backward, it makes it easier to execute in the normal position.)

Coaching Points. This drill is extremely tiring, so limit the time. Monitor how goalkeepers perform saves and look for common mistakes.

Two-Pad Slide Save

The best way to describe this save is to think of a foot-first slide into second base in baseball. To perform this save, goalkeepers must turn their skates into a *T*, push off with the foot farthest from the side they intend to slide toward, and glide with the other. Next, they drop the knee while kicking out the skates and slide across on the hip with the pads stacked on top of each other (see Figure 7.30). Goalies use this save on a quick play around the net or on a breakaway.

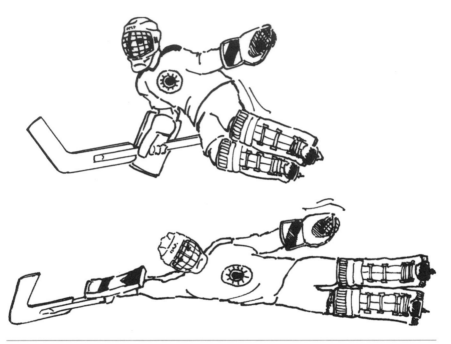

■ **Figure 7.30**   Two-pad slide save.

Two-Pad Slide Drills

Name.   Breakaway in a Controlled Situation

Purpose.   To familiarize goalkeepers with making two-pad slide saves

Organization.   Place a goalkeeper in the net and have several players with pucks/balls go in on breakaways, asking them to deke toward the post at the last minute.

Coaching Point.   Watch for proper technique on each save.

Name.   Quick Play

Purpose.   To familiarize goalkeepers with making two-pad slide saves

Organization.　Have one player pass across the net to another, then take a shot (quick play; see Figure 7.31).

Coaching Point.　Watch for proper technique on each save.

Variation.　Add a third player in front of the net in the high slot so that goalies cannot commit to a two-pad slide.

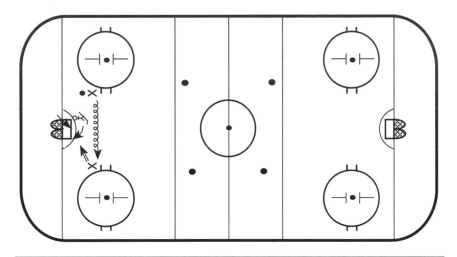

■ **Figure 7.31**　Quick Play Drill.

Glove Saves

Goalkeepers can use the pads and gloves to protect the upper portion of the net rather well if they stay in the ready position. Overall, goalies will be more comfortable with the gloves than the pads, and they usually favor the catching glove over the blocker, which is worn on the hand holding the stick.

Goalkeepers use the catch glove as if it were a baseball glove, following the puck/ball into the glove and squeezing firmly (see Figure 7.32). The biggest mistake inexperienced goalies make is trying to catch too much. They come across the body with the catch glove, which brings them out of the ready position. They also try to catch everything down by the feet, which brings them even farther out of the ready position and puts the head down. Remind goalkeepers always to follow the puck/ball into the glove.

To use the blocker proficiently takes a little more time, but if goalkeepers think of it as an extension of the stick, they may master proper technique easily. Goalies should follow the puck/ball into the blocker and direct it into a corner away from the net. They should not swipe at the puck/ball. Goalkeepers should also be aware of the angle at which the blocker hits the puck/ball. If the angle is too great, the puck/ball will pop up into the air. Goalies should learn to trap on the blocker with the catch glove by placing the catch glove on top of the blocker once the blocker makes contact with the puck/ball.

■ **Figure 7.32**   Glove save.

Glove Save Drill

Name. Big Target

Purpose.   To familiarize goalkeepers with making glove saves

Organization.   Put goalkeepers on the knees, provide a big target, and have players shoot high to either side.

Coaching Point.   Begin by using soft tennis balls or rolled up socks to reduce goalies' fear of being hit. Have players shoot wide to force goalies to move to make saves.

Variations.   At first, allow goalkeepers to try blocker saves without the stick. Toss pucks/balls for trapping practice. Use tennis balls and a tennis ball machine in the beginning. Do off-surface training with only the gloves on.

Error Detection and Correction for Glove Saves	
ERROR	CORRECTION
1. Pulling up out of fear	1. Use soft tennis balls or rolled up socks and graduate to pucks/balls once confidence becomes greater.
2. Inadequate lateral movement into the shot	2. Practice T-push or side-step maneuvers.
3. Giving rebounds out in front of the net off stick glove	3. Snap the wrist and angle the blocker to the corners.
4. Coming across the body with opposite side glove	4. Do not cross the midline of the body with any glove.
5. Taking eyes off the puck/ball	5. Concentrate on the puck/ball and not the shooter.

Playing the Angles

The most important skill for goalkeepers to learn is the art of playing the angles: cutting down on the amount of net the shooter sees behind the goalie. Goalkeepers' best strategy is to avoid sitting back in the net. On a regular shot goalies must come out, stay square to the shooter, and play the puck/ball, not the shooter. If the puck/ball is out in front of the net, goalkeepers may come out, but if the puck/ball is to the side or behind the net, they must stay in the net.

▬▬▬ Angle Drills ▬▬▬

Name. Group Angles

Purpose. To familiarize goalkeepers with judging angles

Organization. Goalkeepers or other players stand directly behind a puck/ball in front of the net (see Figure 7.33). You call out the name of a player as a goalie moves across the net from post to post. The goalkeeper comes out and cuts down the angle, then the player tells the goalkeeper what the player sees behind the goalie. Once the goalie is in the best position to defend the shot, the player shoots.

Coaching Point. Watch goalkeepers' angles. Remember that judging angles looks a lot easier than it is.

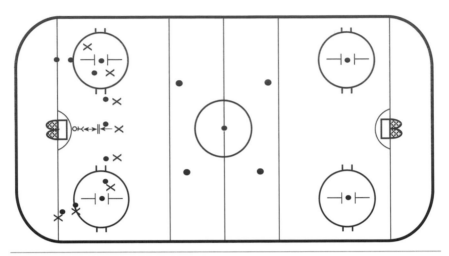

■ **Figure 7.33** Group Angles Drill.

Name. Ropes

Purpose. To familiarize goalkeepers with judging angles

Organization. Tie a rope to the bottom of each post. Pull the rope out to the location of the puck/ball, creating a shooting triangle.

Coaching Points. Watch how goalkeepers execute glove saves and look for common mistakes.

Breakaway Saves

The key to effective defense against breakaways is timing. Teach goalkeepers these basic steps for mastering breakaways: (a) come out extra far; (b) back up with the shooter no deeper than the top of the crease; and (c) make the save (possibly with a two-pad slide). Try not to make the first move. Goalkeepers must learn to time their backward movements and to react to the shooter.

Screen Shot Saves

Teach goalkeepers to defend screen shots by getting low and fighting the screen persistently. The ideal save is the butterfly.

The best way to practice defending against screen shots is to use a screen-shot board. You can make one with a sheet and some framing boards. Design the board so that a puck/ball shot under the sheet on one side cannot be seen by goalies on the other side until the last minute.

Deflections

If goalkeepers feel that a deflection is possible, they must move toward the deflection without losing the angle of the initial shot, then turn and square off to the deflection.

Covering Up the Puck/Ball—Hunger

When a puck/ball is loose in front of the net, the goalie must react quickly to "pounce" on it (cover it up). The analogy of a hungry tiger pouncing on a piece of meat illustrates this save technique.

Error Detection and Correction for Covering Up the Puck/Ball	
ERROR	CORRECTION
1. Failing to keep the head up	1. Keep the head up at all times.
2. Using the stick for protection	2. Cover the puck/ball with the catch glove only. Place the stick and blocker in front of the catch glove once the puck/ball is covered to protect the glove hand from the players' sticks.

Puck/Ball Behind the Net Saves

Teach goalkeepers to use this procedure when the puck/ball goes behind the net. First, as shooters move behind the net, goalies should move to the side post closest to the shooter, remain square, and turn the head in the direction of the shooter. Once the shooter reaches the middle of the back of the net (the safest spot), the goalie must quickly move across the net (T-push) and cover the other side post. The goalie must be ready for a quick pass from behind the net and a wrap-around shot.

Two-On-One and Three-On-Two Saves

On an odd-player rush (two-on-one or three-on-two), the goalie's main responsibility is the shooter. If a late pass is made to the open player, the two-pad slide is usually the save of choice. Any player coming out of the corner provides the toughest play goalkeepers have to handle.

Goalkeepers need to know their limits, simplifying decisions by making a mark on the rink surface at their maximum poke checking point. When poke checking, goalkeepers should neither go down nor lunge the shoulders forward, sacrificing lateral mobility.

As shooters approach, goalkeepers should come out at them (not leaving the post too early), force them to take as much time as possible, and move them into defenders. The wider a shooter goes, the better. Remind goalkeepers that players on their forehand move across the net more easily and have more angle, but are also more vulnerable to a poke check because the puck/ball is out in front. Also remind goalkeepers that players on their backhand can shield the puck/ball better and are less vulnerable to a poke check. Teach goalies that a fake poke check often forces a player away from the net.

In a two-on-one a goalkeeper's job is to take away the short side, and in a two-on-one out of the corner, players will often pass rather than carry the puck/ball out. Goalkeepers should not allow that pass to come through their reach limits!

Face-Offs

If shooters are on their forehand, goalkeepers should line up with the face-off. But if shooters are on their backhand, goalies should either line up with gunners or know where gunners are and be able to get there.

General Rules (Easy Angle Rule)

- Face the puck/ball and shooters.

- Line up so that the puck/ball hits them in the middle of the chest, with shoulders square to the puck/ball, requiring them to move only half of the body to make any save.

- Position themselves in the middle of the shooters' line-of-sight angles and move out to the top of the crease, taking away the net that shooters can see. Get set and avoid moving too far.

- Make themselves look big, avoid covering up equipment that is covering a piece of the net, and always try to cover an open piece of the net.

- Point skates at shooters and try to move a half step behind the puck/ball.

- Make opponents shoot to the side of the net that goalkeepers are approaching, not the side they are leaving, and make the save easy on themselves.

- Control the puck/ball and control play around them so that they know where opponents are. They should play the four segments of the net and read shooters on all plays, including breakaways.

Goalkeepers should learn these maneuvers at a slow pace, then progress to a more rapid pace as their skills improve. Teach them that technique is more important than quickness in the beginning.

If you are lucky to have two goalies, use the second goalie like you would use a video camera. Being able to see the open areas and the amount of net available, will help them when it is their turn at goalie. Remember, the day is over when the overweight player who couldn't skate played goalie. Work with your goalies every chance you get. The entire team will benefit from it!

Communication in Critical Situations

Two-on-one

Goalkeepers need to play the person with the puck/ball. Goalies should talk with the defense on and off the rink surface to ensure mutual understanding.

Back door situations

The numerous defensive coverage exchanges and the need for quick decisions often allow a player to sneak free on the back door. Goalkeepers need to let the team know.

Screens

Goalkeepers must talk with their teammates on and off the rink surface.

Quick breakouts

Because defensive players cannot always see what is going on behind them, goalkeepers need to communicate.

All other situations

When the puck/ball is at the offensive end, goalkeepers should not fall asleep. They should keep track of game time, watch penalty time winding down, and monitor where breakouts develop. Goalies need to remember that they can see many things that the rest of the team cannot. They need to communicate what they see and be positive to maintain the team's motivation.

Unit 8

How Do I Get My Players to Play as a Team?

Understanding hockey and individual skills and drills is important, but hockey is a team sport, and this unit helps you teach individuals to play as a team. Many coaches like to say, "There is no *I* in Team": If players follow this motto, they are more likely to play successful *team* hockey.

We divide team play into three major categories:

- Offensive play (including power plays)
- Defensive play (including penalty killing)
- Transitions

Teach players that when their team has the puck/ball, they all play offense, and when the *opposition* has the puck/ball, they all play defense. Because a primary goal of hockey is to score more goals than the opponent, teach players to put all effort into scoring a goal when they have the puck/ball and to put all effort into getting the puck/ball back when the other team has it.

Communication

The key to a team's ability to play together is communication, on and off the rink surface.

Although communication is an essential team concept, young players sometimes lack the skill to communicate effectively. For example, wanting the puck/ball, players may stop and bang the stick on the rink surface. If they fail to receive a pass, they might bang the stick harder. You can avoid these poor communication attempts by teaching your players more effective strategies.

Verbal Communication

The easiest way to communicate is to talk. However, during a game the other team will hear, too. Teach your players to use verbal communication primarily during stoppages of play. For example, players can use the break just before a face-off to plan a strategy. If a player is always open on the left side, that player can also use the lull before a face-off to inform a teammate.

Another good time to communicate is just after players come off the surface for a line change. Show your players how to use this bench time to discuss the last shift and plan for the next one. Also ensure that your players know how to listen, the most important part of communicating. One hockey coach tells his players, "You were born with two ears and one mouth. Listen twice as much as you speak, and you will have an illustrious hockey career."

Throughout the game, players should also listen closely to goalkeepers, especially when skating the puck/ball out from the defensive end. Goalies are the only players with a wide view of the open surface ahead of play. They can usually see who is open and whether the opposition is setting up on the weak or strong side.

Nonverbal Communication

Players can also use *nonverbal* communication: body language. Players already use nonverbal communication in deking techniques, sending false messages to opponents by faking a move with the puck/ball one way, then following through in a different direction. Encourage them to use it with their teammates, too. The best body parts for nonverbal communication are the eyes. Some say the eyes are the windows to the soul; in hockey they are the windows to the play book. Players should try to make eye contact with a teammate before attempting a pass, ensuring that player is ready. An opponent's eyes can also be revealing. It is hard, for example, to hide fear and uncertainty.

Remember, though, that players will have some difficulty making eye contact through the cage that protects the face. Players should not attempt to remove safety equipment to make eye contact. Nodding the head can be an effective substitute if players are unable to make eye contact. Opponents may also point their sticks, communicating areas where they want to skate or pass. To use nonverbal communication effectively, coaches must make sure that all the players interpret messages accurately. For example, a team could establish a signal that if players point in a specific direction for a pass, they actually want it in the opposite direction. Be creative, but be consistent.

Offensive Concepts

"What was the score?" is the most commonly asked question about a game. This section deals with the scoring aspects of hockey, that part of the game that generates the most excitement from players and fans alike. Teach these basic concepts to your players and have them filling the net:

1. Make the goalie move, opening holes for shooting.
2. Increase scoring productivity.
3. Use one-on-one tactics.
4. Read and react to teammates and opponents.

Making the Goalie Move

The number one strategy players use to score goals is moving the puck/ball, and forcing the goaltender to move. To execute this concept, players set up a play on one side of the net, then pass the puck/ball to the other side for a shot on net. To set up the play, your team enters the offensive zone in an attack triangle (see Figures 8.1a-b). As players move, the attack triangle allows for support on all sides. For example, if player *A* in Figure 8.1a moves to a high position, then player *A* becomes the high support to the low players *B* and *C* (see Figure 8.1b). Initially, *A* was the low player with support from *B* and *C*, but movement of any player changes everyone's responsibility. In five-on-five ice hockey the last two players become the final support of the triangle, forming a second triangle with one player from the first triangle (see Figure 8.2a). In four-on-four roller hockey the last player into the zone forms a second triangle on the opposite side of the rink (see Figure 8.2b). As players take control of the offensive zone, they try to spread out at least one of the triangles, attempting to move the goalkeeper across the net and create the best scoring opportunity (see Figure 8.3). The object of offensive play is to create high-percentage scoring opportunities. If you develop players' creativity through drills and tactics that create time and space, your team will enjoy more scoring opportunities.

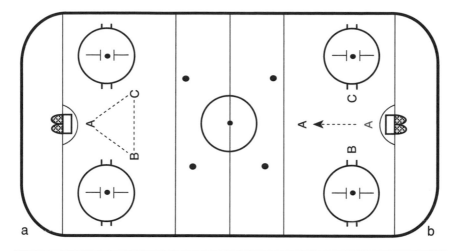

■ **Figure 8.1** Attack triangle: (a) initial setup and (b) movement.

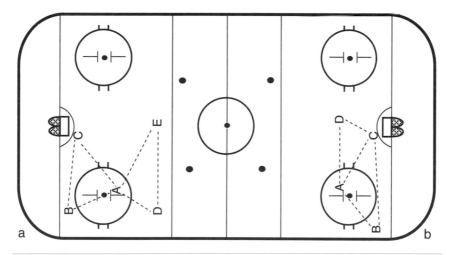

■ **Figure 8.2** (a) Ice hockey (five-on-five) secondary triangle and (b) roller hockey (four-on-four) secondary triangle.

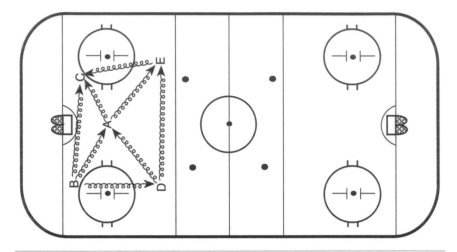

■ Figure 8.3 Forcing goaltender movement to create scoring opportunity.

Increasing Scoring Productivity

To increase scoring productivity, teach your players these six keys.

1. Players should anticipate and react by monitoring the goaltender's position, their own positions, puck/ball location, and opponents' and teammates' positions. They should look at the net before shooting and adjust the shot according to the goalie's position.

2. When in traffic, players should concentrate on shooting or creating an opportunity. Teach your players not to shoot the puck/ball when they lack good opportunities or when another player is open and in a better shooting position.

3. Players should use effective positioning to move into openings at the instant the puck/ball arrives. This concept takes some practice and a little creative skating; puck/ball races or one-on-one reverses are the best ways to improve these skills.

4. Players need to be determined. They should overcome defenders' efforts at preventing them from driving to the net, be ready

for rebounds and loose pucks/balls, and avoid turning away after taking a shot on net. Some players have made it to the NHL largely because they could stand in front of the net and put rebounds in for goals. If players turn away after a shot that fails to score, they are by default giving the puck/ball to the opponents.

5. During one-on-ones, players should be unpredictable and develop a variety of dekes and shots. Players make opponents' jobs easy if they make the same move every time they go down the rink surface. Encourage your players to be creative and have fun.

6. Players should release the puck/ball quickly after receiving passes or making dekes. Players should avoid wasting great dekes or passes across the net by allowing the defensive team—especially the goalkeeper—to set up and react.

Using One-On-One Tactics

Help your players develop good one-on-one tactics, like change of pace skating with and without the puck/ball, inside–out and outside–in skating dekes, and dekes using the head, upper body, and lower body. Also develop tactics like faking shots, looking away prior to passing or shooting, driving to the net both before and after the initial shot, walkouts, and delaying. All these tactics create offensive advantages and more goals.

Reading and Reacting

Finally, you should help your players develop the ability to read and react to changing rink scenarios. The puck/ball carrier must read open rink surface, defensive pressure, and passing options and execute tactics like those discussed previously. Teach your supporting players to decide whether to back up the puck/ball carrier, create a passing option, set a screen, or help create a numerical advantage. Also teach your players who is responsible for each of these options.

Offensive Drills

Name. Puck/Ball Obstacle Course

Purpose. To practice stick handling maneuvers

Organization. Divide players into three groups, and assign each group to a different obstacle. Course A players skate with pucks/balls around a row of pylons and finish with a shot on net. Course B players skate with pucks/balls to a stick lying on the surface, maneuver around the stick and through the two cones, and finish with a shot on net. Course C players negotiate a puck/ball through the legs of a chair and finish with a shot on net (see Figure 8.4). Players stay in their groups, and groups rotate to a different course every 5 to 6 minutes.

Coaching Point. By the second time players attempt the course, ensure that they skate with their heads up.

Variation. Vary speed and intensity.

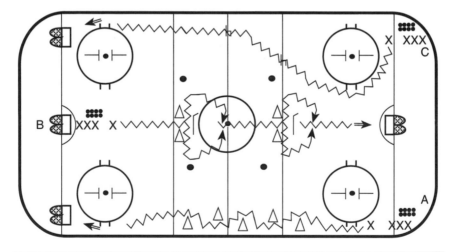

■ **Figure 8.4** Puck/Ball Obstacle Course Drill.

Name. One-On-Zero Around the Circles

Purpose. To practice stick handling maneuvers and driving to the net

Organization. Place a group of players on both sides of the rink in the corners. Players skate out of the corner, receive a pass from the same corner, then skate around the circle and shoot on net.

Next, players proceed to the next circle, receive a pass from the opposite corner, skate that circle, and finish with a shot on net.

Coaching Points. Monitor how players accept the pass and drive to the net, as well as whether they stop skating just before shooting.

Variation. Run the drill forward and backward.

Name.   Box Pass Drill

Purpose. To practice puck/ball movement around the perimeter in the offensive zone

Organization. Place four players inside the offensive zone in a box formation (see Figure 8.5a). The player deep in the corner passes the puck/ball directly in front to another player, then skates out of the zone and around the center face-off dot. While this player skates, the puck/ball is passed around the perimeter, and when the first player skates down the center slot area, the puck/ball is passed to that player for a quick shot on net.

Coaching Points. Ensure that players keep the puck/ball in the offensive zone and that shooting players use a quick release after the pass.

Variation. Pass and Follow Drill. Same drill, but instead of skating around the center face-off dot after passing the puck/ball, the passer follows the pass to the position of the player passed to (see Figure 8.5b). Play continues around the box in this manner until the last player in the box takes the pass, makes a shot on net, and goes to the end of the line.

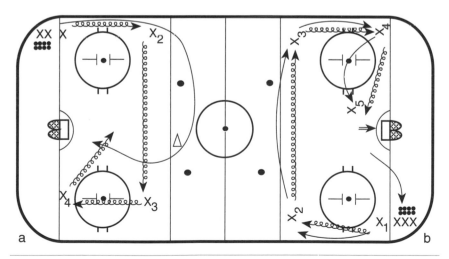

■ **Figure 8.5**   (a) Box Pass Drill and (b) Pass and Follow Drill.

Defensive Concepts

Teach your team these basic defensive concepts to help them prevent opponents from having scoring opportunities:

1. Pressure the puck/ball.
2. Read and react.
3. Cover in front of the net.
4. Cover the points.

Pressuring the Puck/Ball

As soon as your team loses the puck/ball, one of your players should cover the puck/ball carrier, which is called *pressuring*. Players produce this pressure by cutting off puck/ball carriers' skating lanes, angling them into the boards, and taking away their skating surface, forcing them either to give up the puck/ball or to try to pass to a teammate (see Figure 8.6). Ice hockey rules permit checking, but at younger levels and in roller hockey, players must use the stick check or steal the puck/ball off opponents' sticks.

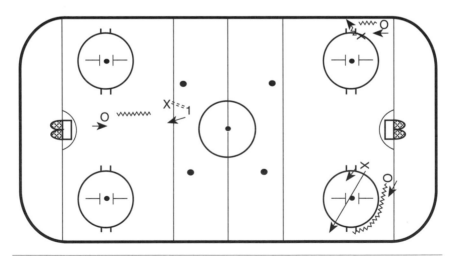

■ **Figure 8.6**　Pressuring the puck/ball: cutting off puck/ball carrier's skating space by angling the player into the boards.

Reading and Reacting

Once your team loses the puck/ball, players quickly assume the defensive mode, assess the situation, and attack. As in pressuring the puck/ball, players attack the puck/ball carrier first, then read and react to other players and the opponents' game plan. The closest teammate must pressure the puck/ball with defensive support. This player follows the lead of the puck/ball pressure and reacts to the action of the puck/ball carrier, looking to intercept the pass. If the opponent reaches the defensive zone, players need to force the play to the outer portion of the zone, keeping the opposition, especially the puck/ball carrier, as close to the boards as possible.

Covering in Front of the Net

The opponent's offense will try to set up someone in front of your net to help with screens and try tip ins. One of your defensive players must stay on this player in front of the net, keeping a body between the net and the offensive player's body. Remember, though, that some coaches believe that the defense should not go after the puck/ball carrier behind the net, preparing instead for a pass or attempt to carry the puck/ball out.

Covering the Points

The other important coverage in the defensive zone—especially in a five-on-five contest—is covering the points (covering the opponent's defense person out by the blue line), trying to stop the point person from taking slapshots. Remember that you are trying to regain the puck/ball before opponents enter your defensive zone and to prevent a quality shot on net. Players must be ready for the point player to deke and go around the coverage.

Defensive Drills

Name. One-On-One in a Confined Space

Purpose. To practice offensive and defensive maneuvers in a confined space

Organization. Place two players inside a face-off circle. One player receives a puck/ball, and the other tries to strip it away (see Figure 8.7). If the defense gets the puck/ball, roles reverse. Time each group and have a second group ready while the previous group rests.

Coaching Points. Monitor puck/ball protection and defensive skills.

Variations. Vary intensity. Also, run as a two-on-one and two-on-two in a confined space.

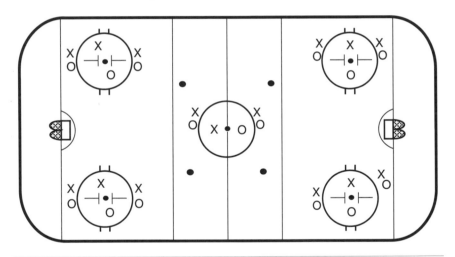

■ **Figure 8.7** One-On-One in a Confined Space Drill.

Name. Puck/Ball Races Into the Corners

Purpose. To practice defensive maneuvers and forcing the puck/ball carrier deep

Organization. You can run this drill simultaneously in all four zones. Place players 5 to 10 feet apart, about even with the offside face-off circles. Designate one player offense and the other defense. As you give the command, shoot a puck/ball into the corner, signaling players to race to the puck/ball and play a mini one-on-one. The defensive player tries to force the offensive player wide and cut off the skating lane as the offensive player tries to break to the net and score (see Figure 8.8).

Coaching Point. Monitor offensive skills one time and defensive skills another time.

Variations. Start players in different positions (sitting, on the knees, back, or buttocks). Start players at different intervals to give a specific concept an advantage.

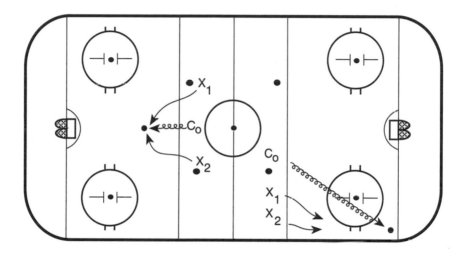

Figure 8.8 Puck/Ball Races Into the Corners Drill.

The Transition Game

How quickly your players transfer thoughts and actions from offense to defense, and vice versa, will dramatically affect your team's success. Ideally, ice hockey transitions from defense to offense occur in the neutral zone, and roller hockey transitions occur between the tops of the face-off circles. Teach two primary transition concepts to your players: countering and regrouping.

Countering

If you can *counter* faster than your opponent can organize its attack, your team will have a good chance to regain the puck/ball quickly. Countering incorporates the element of surprise and relies on quickness to catch your opponents off guard.

Regrouping

After regaining the puck/ball with a successful counter, players must quickly *regroup* the team and set the offense in action. If players regroup faster than opponents counter, the team has many *odd-player rushes* (your offense outnumbers the opponent's defense), and odd-player rushes help you score goals.

To help players visualize the transition concept, tell them to picture offense and defense as opposite ends of a light switch. Players should strive to make transitions in the time it takes to flip the switch. Players make transitions mentally and physically, either attacking the puck/ball carrier and scrambling into prescribed defensive positions or trying to move the puck/ball toward the offensive end, scrambling into the attack triangle.

Power Plays

A *power play* occurs when an opponent allows your team to gain a numerical advantage, usually after a penalty. Your power-play unit, consisting of the players you decide to have on the surface during the power play, should be directed by a quarterback—the player best able to read the defense—and should be extremely quick. Before your first game, you need to develop a team philosophy for the power play: Will you use your best players or keep your same player rotation? One approach is to hold tryouts for the power play and short-handed (penalty-killing) units on your team. Develop three to four different units, and practice with them all. Your power-play unit needs good passing and receiving skills: Emphasize one-touch passing, shooting, deflection, and tip ins, and position a player in front of the net who is a scoring threat. Teach your power-play units to

1. create and master the two-on-one,
2. spread out the defense and move to open surface without the puck/ball,
3. develop good individual skills, and
4. address problems as they occur.

Your power-play unit should be able to read the defense, control the puck/ball, and continually move the puck/ball and opponents toward the net. If possible, practice your power-play unit against your penalty-killing unit or reserve players.

Creating and Mastering the Two-On-One

If your team outnumbers the defense two-on-one, seek a quality scoring opportunity. Teach players to stagger themselves, making it harder for the defense to cover them and forcing the goalkeeper to cover a player—usually the shooter. Also teach players to fake the shoot and pass the puck/ball off the deke. Remember that the defense is trying to split your two players and force the puck/ball carrier to the outside: Prevent defenders from succeeding.

Spreading Out the Defense and Moving to Open Surface Without the Puck/Ball

During a power play, prevent defenders from covering two of your players with one of theirs. Teach players to spread out the defense by passing the puck/ball around the perimeter of the offensive zone. This allows your players to weave in and out of the space between defenders. By doing this an offensive player can be passed the puck/ball while wide open in the middle of the defense which can create quality scoring opportunities.

Developing Good Individual Skills

Power-play plans will only succeed if players are proficient in the basic skills such as passing and shooting the puck/ball accurately, making one-touch passes, and shooting off a direct pass. As your team's proficiency in the basic skills increases, so also will the effectiveness of their power plays.

Addressing Problems as They Occur

One of the most common problems underlying ineffective power-play units is that players stand still, not moving the puck/ball. Power plays require almost constant motion. Standing still also prevents players from getting to the loose puck/ball. You can avoid this problem by allowing better skilled, quicker players to carry the puck/ball up the surface, quarterbacking the power-play unit. Not winning face-offs, especially in the offensive end, also causes problems: If you do not have the puck/ball, you cannot score a goal. Another problem is abandoning the attack triangle philosophy, preventing players from taking advantage of three-on-twos and support techniques. Finally, if players do not take what the opposition gives them, the power play will not succeed. Keep in mind that players frequently get in trouble by signaling their intentions, allowing the defense to prepare; teach them to read and react!

Penalty Killing

A *penalty-killing unit* may be called on 6 to 15 times in a single game. You need to decide whether to prepare a specific group of players for this special situation. Very young players need to experience a variety of opportunities, but more advanced levels may increase the need to specialize.

Good penalty-killing units should possess similar skills as power-play units. Instead of focusing on scoring, though, these units focus on defending against the power play. A good penalty-killing unit should be able to read and react to the opposition, applying defensive skills effectively. One key to an effective penalty-killing unit is a good face-off person: To control the opposition, your team must get the puck/ball. The penalty-killing unit should also be able to block shots and control play in front of its own net. Players should be quick, but patient. Because you are a player down, the team must wait for an opportunity, then seize it.

When your five-on-five ice hockey team is a player down, select from two basic formations: *box formation* and *diamond formation* (see Figure 8.9a–b). The disadvantage of the box formation is that the box can be collapsed by the opponent's offense, leading to an unorganized defense at a very vulnerable time. The disadvantage of the diamond formation is that one player has to cover the opponent's two point players, probably leading to several long shots on net. However, if that player is your quickest and smartest, the team will also have a chance at a few shorthanded breakaways. In five-on-three ice hockey and four-on-three roller hockey (when your team is down two players), the only formation to play is a triangle (see

Figure 8.10). Keep the base of the triangle down by the net, as it represents the highest percentage scoring area for the opposition. The final formation, four-on-two roller hockey, leaves your team with only two players to defend the entire surface. Your best chance is an alert goaltender and two players who are as fast as lightning. Your two players each try to cover half of the surface, usually right and left, but opponents frequently win this battle.

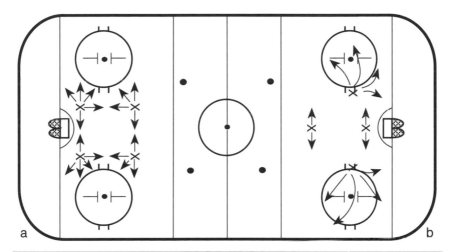

■ **Figure 8.9** Penalty-killing formations: (a) box formation and (b) diamond formation.

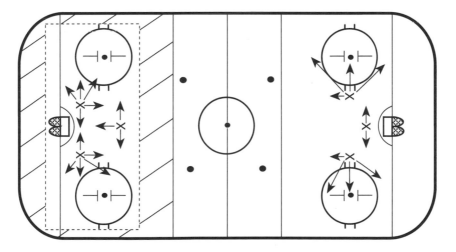

■ **Figure 8.10** Triangle penalty-killing formation (five-on-three or four-on-three).

When a penalty-killing unit gets control of the puck/ball, it has two choices: clear the puck/ball all the way down the surface (icing is negated for a penalized team during the penalty) or try to control it by spreading out and using crisp, sharp passes, trying to play keepaway from the opposition. Depending on the opponent's momentum and the area in which your team recovers the puck/ball, each is an effective tool in killing penalties. Just remember to practice!

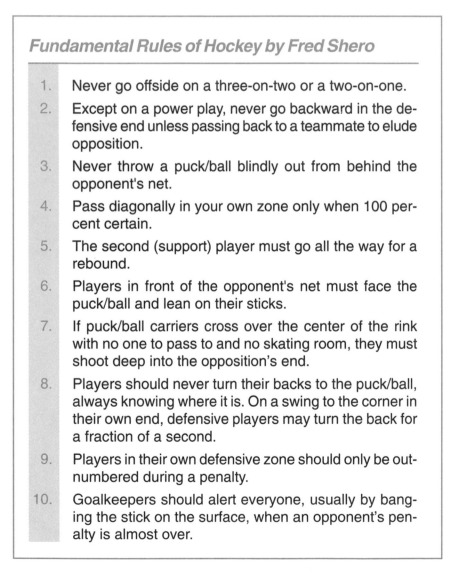

Fundamental Rules of Hockey by Fred Shero

1. Never go offside on a three-on-two or a two-on-one.
2. Except on a power play, never go backward in the defensive end unless passing back to a teammate to elude opposition.
3. Never throw a puck/ball blindly out from behind the opponent's net.
4. Pass diagonally in your own zone only when 100 percent certain.
5. The second (support) player must go all the way for a rebound.
6. Players in front of the opponent's net must face the puck/ball and lean on their sticks.
7. If puck/ball carriers cross over the center of the rink with no one to pass to and no skating room, they must shoot deep into the opposition's end.
8. Players should never turn their backs to the puck/ball, always knowing where it is. On a swing to the corner in their own end, defensive players may turn the back for a fraction of a second.
9. Players in their own defensive zone should only be outnumbered during a penalty.
10. Goalkeepers should alert everyone, usually by banging the stick on the surface, when an opponent's penalty is almost over.

Appendix A

Organizations to Contact for Coaching Children With Disabilities

American Athletic Association of the Deaf
3607 Washington Boulevard, Suite 4
Ogden, UT 84403-1737
(801) 393-8710
TTY: (801) 393-7916
Fax: (801) 393-2263

Disabled Sports USA
451 Hungerford Drive, Suite 100
Rockville, MD 20850
(301) 217-0960

Paralyzed Veterans of America
801 18th Street NW
Washington, DC 20006
(202) 872-1300
(800) 424-8200

Special Olympics International
1325 G Street NW, Suite 500
Washington, DC 20005
(202) 628-3630

U.S. Association of Blind Athletes
33 North Institute
Colorado Springs, CO 80903
(719) 630-0422

U.S. Cerebral Palsy Athletic Association
3810 West NW Highway, Suite 205
Dallas, TX 75220
(214) 351-1510

U.S. Les Autres Sports Association
1475 West Gray, Suite 166
Houston, TX 77019-4926
(713) 521-3737

Appendix B

Sample Season Plan for Beginning Ice and Roller Hockey Players

Goal: To help players learn and practice the individual skills and team tactics needed to play hockey games successfully.

T(#) = Initial skill teaching time (minutes)   * = Skills practiced during drills and activities
P(#) = Review and practice time (minutes)

Skills	Week 1		Week 2		Week 3		Week 4	
	Day 1	Day 2	Day 1	Day 2	Day 1	Day 2	Day 1	Day 2
Warm-Up Exercises	T(10)	P(10)	P(10)	P(10)	P(10)	P(10)	P(10)	P(10)
Cool-Down Exercises	T(10)	P(5)	P(5)	P(5)	P(5)	P(5)	P(5)	P(5)
Evaluation	(5)	(5)	(5)	(5)	(5)	(5)	(5)	(5)
Fundamentals								
Rink geography	T(10)	T(10)	T(10)	T(10)	P(5)	P(5)	P(5)	P(5)
Rules	T(5)	T(5)	T(5)	T(5)	T(5)	T(5)	*	*
Skating								
Forward	T(15)	P(10)	P(15)	P(10)	*	*	*	*
Starting	T(5)	P(5)	P(5)	P(5)	*	*	*	*
Stopping	T(5)	P(5)	P(5)	P(5)	*	*	*	*
Turning		T(10)	P(5)	P(5)	*	*	*	*
Pivoting			T(10)	P(10)	P(5)	P(5)	P(5)	*
Backward			T(10)	P(10)	P(5)	P(5)	*	*
Drills				P(15)	P(10)		P(10)	P(10)

	Week 1		Week 2		Week 3		Week 4	
Skills *(continued)*	Day 1	Day 2	Day 1	Day 2	Day 1	Day 2	Day 1	Day 2
Puck Handling								
Stationary stick handling			T(5)	P(5)	*	*	*	*
Stick handling with movement				T(5)	P(5)		P(5)	*
Passing								
Forehand and backhand				T(10)	P(10)	P(5)	*	*
Flip passing					T(5)	P(5)	P(5)	*
Receiving				T(10)	P(10)	P(10)	P(5)	*
Drills					P(10)	P(10)		P(10)
Shooting								
Forehand				T(5)	P(5)	P(5)	*	*
Backhand				T(5)	P(5)	P(5)	*	*
Snap shots					T(5)	P(5)	P(5)	*
Flip shots					T(5)	P(5)	P(5)	*
Drills						P(10)		P(10)
Checking								
Stick checking					T(5)	P(10)	P(10)	P(10)
Lifting the stick					T(5)	P(10)	P(10)	P(10)
Covering the opponent			T(5)		T(5)	P(10)	P(10)	P(10)
Drills			P(10)		P(10)		P(10)	P(10)

(continued)

Skills (continued)	Week 1 Day 1	Week 1 Day 2	Week 2 Day 1	Week 2 Day 2	Week 3 Day 1	Week 3 Day 2	Week 4 Day 1	Week 4 Day 2
Goaltending								
Stance and movement			T(5)	*	*	*	*	*
Skate saves			T(5)	P(5)	P(5)	P(5)	P(5)	*
Pad saves			T(5)	P(5)	P(5)	P(5)	P(5)	*
Stick saves				T(5)	P(5)	P(5)	P(5)	P(5)
Poke checks				T(5)	P(5)	P(5)	P(5)	P(5)
Glove saves					T(5)	P(5)	P(5)	P(5)
Playing angles					T(5)	P(5)	P(5)	P(5)
Special saves					T(5)	P(5)	P(5)	P(5)
Drills					P(15)	P(10)	P(15)	P(10)
Team Offense								
One-on-one tactics							T(10)	P(10)
Making the goalie move								T(10)
Reading and reacting								
Drills								
Team Defense								
Pressing the puck								T(10)
Reading and reacting								
Covering								
Drills								
Special Teams								
Power plays								
Penalty killing								

Appendix C

Ice and Roller Hockey Referee Signals

Boarding
Striking the closed fist of the hand once into the open palm of the other hand.

Butt-Ending
Moving the forearm, fist closed, under the forearm of the other hand held palm down.

Charging
Rotating clenched fists around one another in front of chest.

Checking From Behind
Arm placed behind the back, elbow bent, forearm parallel to the surface.

Clearing—Roller Hockey Icing—Ice Hockey Offsides
Extending the free arm (without whistle) over the head.

Cross-Checking
A forward motion with both fists clenched extending from the chest.

Delayed Calling of Penalty—Ice Hockey
The non-whistle hand is extended straight above the head.

Delayed Calling of Penalty—Roller Hockey
(penalty in one-referee system) Referee raises arm to upright position. At stoppage of play, points with free hand (free of whistle) with palm open and fingers together.

Delaying the Game
The non-whistle hand, palm open, is placed across the chest and then fully extended directly in front of the body.

Elbowing
Tapping the elbow with
the opposite hand.

Fighting (Roughing)
One punching motion to the
side with the arm extending
from the shoulder.

Goal Scored
A single point, with the non-whistle hand,
directly at the goal in which the puck/ball
legally entered, while simultaneously
blowing the whistle.

Hand Pass
The non-whistle hand (open
hand) and arm are placed
straight down alongside the
body and swung forward and up
once in an underhand motion.

High-Sticking
Holding both fists, clenched,
one immediately above the
other, at the side of the head.

Holding
Clasping the wrist of the whistle hand well in front of the chest.

Holding the Face Mask
Closed fist held in front of face, palm in, and pulled down in one straight motion.

Hooking
A tugging motion with both arms, as if pulling something toward the stomach.

Interference
Crossed arms stationary in front of chest with fists closed.

Kneeing
A single tap of the right knee with the right hand, keeping both skates on the surface.

Match Penalty—Ice Hockey
Pat flat of hand on the top of the head.

Misconduct
Placing of both hands
on hips one time.

Penalty Shot
Arms crossed (fists clenched)
above head.

Slashing
One chop of the hand across
the straightened forearm of
the other hand.

Delayed (Slow) Whistle
(blueline offsides)
The non-whistle hand is extended
straight above the head. If play
returns to neutral zone without
stoppage, the arm is drawn down
the instant the puck/ball crosses
the line, or as soon as the
offending team clears the zone.

Spearing
A single jabbing motion with both hands together, thrust forward from in front of the chest, then dropping hands to the side.

Tripping
Strike the side of the knee and follow through once, keeping the head up and both skates on the surface.

Time-Out
Using both hands to form a *T*.

"Wash-Out"
Both arms swung laterally across the body at shoulder level with palms down.
    1. When used by the referee, it means no goal or violation so play shall continue.
    2. When used by linespeople, it means there is no icing, offside, or high-sticking violation.

Skating resources for coaches and players

Laura Stamm's Power Skating

(Second Edition)

Laura Stamm

1989 • Paper • 256 pp • Item PSTA0331
ISBN 0-88011-331-6 • $18.95 ($27.95 Canadian)

"I highly recommend this book for all coaches and players."
  Herb Brooks
  Head Coach, 1980 U.S. Olympic Team
  Former Head Coach, New York Rangers

In-Line Skating

Mark Powell and John Svensson

1993 • Paper • 152 pp • Item PPOW0399
ISBN 0-87322-399-3 • $13.95 ($19.50 Canadian)

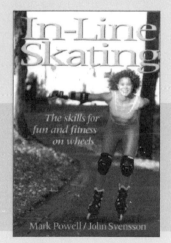

"This book covers it all, from first steps and basic skills to hockey and extreme skating. Skaters at all levels of development and from all disciplines of in-lining will find this a great book to read and reference."
  John Lavelle
  International In-Line Skating Association
  Board of Directors

To place your order, U.S. customers **call TOLL FREE 1 800 747-4457.** Customers outside the U.S. place your order using the appropriate telephone number/address shown in the front of this book.

Human Kinetics
The Premier Publisher for Sports & Fitness

2335

Prices subject to change.

Educational tools for coaches at all levels

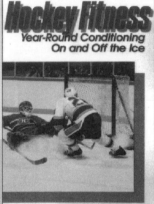

Hockey Fitness

Year-Round Conditioning,
On and Off the Ice

Don MacAdam and
Gail Reynolds

1988 • Paper • 152 pp • Item PMAC0314
ISBN 0-88011-314-6 • $14.95 ($20.95 Canadian)

Learn how to determine players' physical condition, conduct fitness tests, set season objectives, and design a conditioning program.

ASEP Volunteer Level

The American Sport Education Program (ASEP) offers three Volunteer Level curriculums for adults who work with youth sport:

- The **SportCoach** Program consists of the Rookie Coaches Course, which provides inexperienced coaches with essential information for teaching the skills and strategies of a sport, and the Coaching Young Athletes Course, which is for second-year coaches and others who want additional instruction in the principles of coaching.

- The **SportParent** Course is a program that provides youth sport administrators and coaches with a practical and effective way to educate parents about their children's participation in sports.

- The **SportDirector** program offers outstanding opportunities for youth sport directors to improve sport programs for the children in their community. The program includes a very practical *Youth SportDirector Guide* and a dynamic workshop.

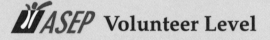

To place your order, U.S. customers **call TOLL FREE 1 800 747-4457**. Customers outside the U.S. place your order using the appropriate telephone number/address shown in the front of this book.

 Human Kinetics
The Premier Publisher for Sports & Fitness

Prices subject to change.

2335